GROWTH
AND WELFARE IN THE
AMERICAN
PAST

GROWTH
AND WELFARE

Douglass C. North
University of Washington

IN THE
AMERICAN
PAST

a new economic history

Prentice-Hall, Inc., Englewood Cliffs, New Jersey

Growth and Welfare in the American Past
Douglass C. North

© Copyright 1966 by Prentice-Hall, Inc.
Englewood Cliffs, N.J.

Library of Congress Catalog Card No.: 66-17371
C 36564 (C)   C 36563 (P)

Current printing (last digit)

10 9 8 7 6 5 4

PRENTICE-HALL INTERNATIONAL, INC.   *London*
PRENTICE-HALL OF AUSTRALIA, PTY. LTD.   *Sydney*
PRENTICE-HALL OF CANADA, LTD.   *Toronto*
PRENTICE-HALL OF INDIA (PRIVATE), LTD.   *New Delhi*
PRENTICE-HALL OF JAPAN, INC.   *Tokyo*

PREFACE

In the past twenty years, American economic history has been undergoing profound change, but the results of this change have not yet brought about a general historical reappraisal, despite their implications for radical revision of the way in which we view our past. The forbidding nature of economic and statistical theory has confined this reappraisal to the professional journals and to the very limited audience of scholars trained in the fields of economic theory and statistics. While this revolution is just beginning, its consequences are already of sufficient magnitude to suggest a basic overhauling of much of our understanding of the past. Some results serve primarily to challenge existing interpretations and to point the way toward further research that may uncover alternative explanations. Other implications are that traditional major problems or issues are not really problems or issues at all. And still other new findings suggest alternative answers widely at variance with existing interpretations.

A primary objective of this book is to present a nontechnical reappraisal of America's economic experience, weaving together the summary results of our new quantitative knowledge of America's past with reappraisal of a number of basic issues and interpretations. However, there is something even more fundamental at stake here. The new economic history points the way to a basic restructuring of historical inquiry. If history is to be something more than a subjective reordering of the facts of the past as man's perspective changes with each generation, we must apply the disciplines of the social sciences to historical research, and apply the methods of scientific inquiry to testing the resultant hypotheses. Economic history is better equipped to pioneer in this approach than are the other social sciences, because of its well-articulated body of theory and the abundance of relevant quantitative data.[1] But the implications and promise for the other social sciences are clear enough. To maintain, as many historians have, that the lack of quantitative data before the nineteenth century renders this approach to history useless is to say only that nothing can be done with earlier periods. Current historical inquiry for earlier periods simply uses implicit (and usually bad) theory and implicit quantitative measurements arrived at by the weight given to the facts presented as evidence. Surely, it is better that the theory be explicit and consistent with the state of theorizing in the discipline and that the implicit quantitative weights be made explicit.

Nothing in what I have said in any way reduces the requirements that the historian be equipped with immense knowledge of his subject matter; nor does it reduce the need for fine detective work in evaluation of historical information, which is the trademark of the first-rate historian. What it does do is impose the additional burden that he be equipped with the relevant theory and knowledge of statistical methods. These are imposing requirements, but the promise is equally impressive.

This study is not a complete economic history of the United States. It necessarily slights the rich descriptive material that should be included in a larger volume, and it concentrates on examining major trends and issues in American economic history. After the first two introductory chapters, each succeeding chapter provides a general descriptive and analytical examination of a period or specific subject and then explores in some detail a major issue in the history of the American economy. It is designed to be a challenge to scholar

---

[1] There is certainly nothing new about this controversy. Historians have been debating about a more scientific history for a long time. But until the social science disciplines were sufficiently developed and some results could be demonstrated, the controversy remained an empty one indeed.

and student, and it will succeed if it promotes (or provokes) their further curiosity and investigation of the methods used and the issues raised herein.

I am indebted to many of my colleagues in economics at the University of Washington whom I have continuously badgered for advice. In particular, Yoram Barzel, Donald Gordon, Walter Oi, and Bob Thomas have contributed valuable suggestions.

Professor Lance E. Davis of Purdue University talked over many of the issues with me and helped to clarify a number of points. I owe a special debt to Professor Robert W. Fogel of the University of Chicago, who read the entire manuscript and made many general and detailed suggestions for improvement, materially contributing to the final result. Lance Davis, Bob Fogel, and my colleagues should be spared any onus for its shortcomings.

The Institute for Economic Research at the University of Washington is a rather special cooperative venture in which I receive the credit that appropriately should be shared with Mary Jane Anderson, Marion T. Olson, and LaDonna Richardson. This manuscript is one more product of their toils, far beyond the requirements of any job, to meet my arbitrary deadlines in spite of the many obstacles I imposed. Phillip Droke did the careful and painstaking work of preparing the charts.

DOUGLASS C. NORTH

ABBREVIATIONS USED IN CITATIONS
OF PUBLISHED WORKS

AER	*American Economic Review*
AHR	*American Historical Review*
EDCC	*Economic Development and Cultural Change*
EHR	*Economic History Review*
GPO	U.S. Government Printing Office
Hist. Statistics	U.S. Bureau of the Census, *Historical Statistics of the United States, Colonial Times to 1957*
ICHS	*The International Congress of the Historical Sciences*
IEAC	International Economic Association Conference
JEH	*Journal of Economic History*
JP	*Journal of Philosophy*
JPE	*Journal of Political Economy*
NBER	National Bureau of Economic Research
SEJ	*Southern Economic Journal*
U.S. Cong. JEC	U.S. Congress Joint Economic Committee

CONTENTS

CHARTS

MAPS

TABLES

chapter 1

THEORY, STATISTICS, AND HISTORY

I

Economic history focuses on two main issues. First, it examines the over-all economic growth, stagnation, or decline of a society. Second, it turns to the question of what happens to people within the society in the course of such growth, stagnation, or decline. The latter issue is a consideration of the relative economic welfare of groups. If, as a society grew richer, everyone's income were to grow at the same rate, this would not be a vital question. But we know that in the course of growth some groups fare better than others. On occasion, even in a prospering society, the income of some parts of the society may actually be dropping.

In examining the American experience, then, we are going to ask the dual question: What factors influenced (1) the rate of growth of the economy, and (2) the well-being of various segments of its society, as the country grew?

In order to talk meaningfully about growth and welfare, it is necessary to use economic theory and statistics. It is impossible to analyze and explain the issues dealt with in economic history without developing initial hypotheses and testing them in the light of available evidence. The initial hypotheses come from the body of

1

economic theory that has evolved in the past 200 years and is being continually tested and refined by empirical inquiry. The statistics provide the precise measurement and empirical evidence by which to test the theory. *The limits of inquiry are dictated by the existence of appropriate theory and evidence.*

Existing economic theory is appropriate for a broad range of issues in economic history dealing with welfare. Since it has already been tested and retested in innumerable empirical inquiries, it is essentially a major short cut distilled from previous research in the initial exploration of the welfare issue at hand. Testing these hypotheses leads to their rejection or modification in the light of the evidence, but the first essential step is drawn from the body of economic theory.

In the study of economic growth, the theory is far from completely adequate. Nevertheless, the development of hypotheses about economic growth in the past twenty years has been a major part of research in economics and has revolutionary implications for reappraisal of all economic history. Future studies of economic growth will surely provide new fuel for the economic historian, but we already have sufficient applicable theory for a start, as the brief distillation in the next section will illustrate.

The evidence is, ideally, statistical data that precisely define and measure the issues to be tested. The immense development of such data in American economic history in the past fifteen years has made possible this revolution in economic history, even though it is still a long way from providing the information necessary, as many of the subsequent chapters will testify. It is a Utopian dream to expect that the economic historian will ever have all the precise quantitative information to test his theories (although diligent digging has yielded, and promises to yield, a much richer mine of it than was expected in both the near and distant past), and here the more imprecise and traditional evidence of the historian found in diaries, records, etc., must be carefully mined. The important point to keep in mind is that it is a rough and crude proxy for precise measurement, and the historian must be self-conscious about the implicit weights he is using in employing such discrete and qualitative information.

II

The reason for the economic historian's concern with the overall growth of society should be apparent. How well-off people can be within a society depends on how much that society produces in the way of goods and services. Going back two hundred years or less, we discover that most people lived poorly (by modern Western standards). Their society simply did not produce enough. It was therefore impossible for more than a very small segment of the population to have high living standards [1]—a condition that still characterizes a good part of the world today. The prime issue to be understood, then, is how in a small part of the world—the Western world—growth has been achieved that makes possible a standard of life that was simply undreamed of in centuries past.

The term economic growth has two distinct meanings. When people say that a city or region grows, they usually mean that the number of people, the amount of business activity, increases. That is, there is an increase in output because more people, capital, and land are being put into productive use. This is commonly called "extensive" growth. It was a major aspect of America's development in the past, in the sense that in the eighteenth and nineteenth centuries the territorial boundaries of the United States were filled out. Millions of people came from foreign shores to help in the process, and foreign capital came as well.

This *extensive* growth resulted in the growth of output of goods and services; but it did not necessarily mean the growth of output *per head*. That is the crucial aspect of growth—and it is the meaning that economists usually employ, because it is concerned with how well-off people are. A society is better off only if it pro-

---

[1] The importance of increasing productive capacity cannot be overemphasized. Redistributing income or eliminating depressions would result in less gain for the poor or the whole society than they would derive from an even relatively short period of sustained economic growth. The consequences of a compounded real per capita growth rate of 1.6 per cent per year dwarf all other welfare effects in our history (assuming no change in income distribution).

duces more *output per person*.[2] This "intensive" growth, or the growth of individual well-being, can come about only if output grows at a more rapid rate than population growth.[3] Before examining the sources of increasing per capita output (and its counterpart, the income people receive for producing that output, or income per capita) it is well to remember that scarcity has been man's oldest problem. By necessity, it has been the dominant feature of life on this planet ever since its beginning. Man has had to eke and scratch out a living throughout most of the known past, and the degree to which he has climbed above a narrow level of subsistence has been limited indeed. Most of history has been a story of man getting just barely enough to live on. But the last three or four centuries have seen a dramatic change in which, in the Western world and particularly in these United States, man has soared above this level. Today, hunger, famine, and subsistence are not major American problems, as they have been for most of man's history and continue to be in many parts of the world. Table 1 shows that the per capita output of most of the world is still very low. The figures on per capita output were reached by taking the total income of each country and dividing by its population to give per capita figures, which were then translated from that country's currency into equivalent dollars. There are many inherent limitations in this method of making intercountry comparisons, but it gives a rough approximation of comparative levels of living and illustrates that a very small percentage of the world lives by a standard that most Americans would consider even crudely comfortable. If a dividing line of $600 annually per head is set as a rough approximation, more than three quarters of the world's population lives below this level, and only the countries of the Western world have greatly bettered it.

What accounts for this phenomenon—that the United States and a small part of the world have been so successful, and the rest

[2] An important alternative is additional leisure. People in a society may choose more leisure in the form of a shorter work week; and the decline in the work week in the United States from approximately 70 hours to a 40-hour week reflects a desire to substitute more leisure for additional output and income.

[3] This suggests the further complication of an increase in population in response to rising income. In many parts of the world there has been a "Malthusian" response to increasing total output, so that output per head has not increased. In America, where people were scarce in relation to land and resources, this was never a problem.

TABLE 1. PER CAPITA OUTPUT IN 1957

(Converted to U.S. dollars by means of foreign exchange rates)

Per capita output	Including 49.7% of world's population	
	Asia and Middle East	**Africa**
	Afghanistan	Angola
	India	Belgian Congo
$0-100	North Korea	Liberia
	Pakistan	Nigeria
	Vietnam (North and South)	Somaliland
		Sudan

	Including 17.1% of world's population	
	Latin America	**Asia and Middle East**
	Brazil	Ceylon
	Colombia	Indonesia
	Guatemala	Iran
	Haiti	Iraq
$101-300	Peru	Philippines
		U.A.R.
	Europe	
	Albania	**Africa**
	Portugal	Algeria
	Spain	Morocco
	Yugoslavia	Tunisia

	Including 18% of world's population	
	Latin America	**Europe**
	Argentina	Bulgaria
	Chile	E. Germany
	Cuba	Greece
	Uruguay	Hungary
$301-600		Ireland
		Italy
	Asia and Middle East	Poland
	Japan	Rumania
	Malaya	U.S.S.R.

	Including 7.5% of world's population	
	Latin America	**Europe (cont.)**
	Venezuela	Czechoslovakia
		Denmark
	Asia and Middle East	France
$601-1200	Israel	W. Germany
		Netherlands
	Europe	Norway
	Austria	United Kingdom
	Belgium	

(table continued on next page)

TABLE 1 (cont.)

Per capita output	Including 7.7 % of world's population		
	America	Europe	Oceania
$1200 and over	United States	Luxemburg	Australia
	Canada	Sweden	New Zealand
		Switzerland	

Source: Everett E. Hagen, "Some Facts about Income Levels and Economic Growth," *Review of Economics and Statistics,* XLII, No. 1 (Feb. 1960), 63.

of the world relatively ineffectual in achieving a high standard of living? This book is a case study of the country that has been most notably successful in this pursuit.

Economic growth essentially means increasing efficiency—that is, what makes a country grow and become better off per head is that it produces more output per person; therefore, when we talk about growth, we are concentrating on what makes a society more efficient. And what makes a society more efficient comprises three main features.

The first of these is technology; the second is investment in people or, to use the economist's term, investment in human capital; and the third is the efficiency of economic organization.

Technology has been the main answer of economic historians in talking about the success of the Western world. The Industrial Revolution has been viewed as a kind of watershed in man's experience; on the far side of it, man was doomed to live at low levels of subsistence, while on the near side, the Industrial Revolution has made possible substantially higher standards of life.

A man of two hundred years ago would have been more at home a thousand years or even fifteen hundred years earlier than he would be in our day. In the past two centuries, man's life has been transformed incalculably by radical changes in technology: (1) the substitution of machines for man's hands to undertake projects—and this is one that Adam Smith made famous in his early discussion in *The Wealth of Nations;* (2) the development of new sources of energy, of which the most famous was the development of the steam engine in the Industrial Revolution period, but more recent examples are the internal combustion engine, the turbine and hydroelectric power, and modern nuclear power; and (3) the dramatic and revolutionary advances in transforming matter to make it useful for mankind, such as transmuting ubiquitous, workaday coal into luxury textiles and fabrics.

A moment's reflection, however, should suggest that this source of growth alone is not a sufficient explanation of the unique experience of the United States, since technological knowledge is free to all. Anyone who wants to use modern technology needs only to read the scientific journals, to borrow from the most advanced countries doing research.[4] Therefore, if technology were the whole story of economic growth, all the countries in the world should be well-off. As a matter of fact, what has happened is that countries have not been able to make efficient use of this technology—that is, they could not reach the potential that is evident in real life in the Western world, and in America particularly—because they lack the other two essentials listed previously: human capital that is capable of adapting, modifying, and using technology, and efficient economic organization.

Modern technology is highly complicated. It requires vast amounts of education or "investment in human capital." First must come the training of engineers and scientists who will modify and adapt it to the particular needs of the different countries; since each country has different resource endowments and different prices at which labor and capital work, what is ideal technology for one country needs modification for another.[5] Second, this technology must be widely employed, requiring a labor force intelligent and educated enough to make efficient use of the machinery and techniques. And third, as society becomes more complex (as in urban industrial economies like the United States in modern times), a vast array of other educated professional people is needed to carry out

---

[4] There is still no over-all theory of technological change, although some interesting hypotheses have emerged in recent research. Note, however, that it is one problem to explain fundamental advances in technology and still another to explain the spread of existing technological knowledge.

[5] For example, a machine is made in America in light of the fact that skilled labor may cost $3.00 an hour; therefore, the machine is designed to economize on labor. Such a machine may not be the most efficient type in India, where labor costs are a small fraction of U.S. costs, but the machine is just as expensive as it is in the United States.

the complex tasks of a highly interrelated society. Most under-developed areas simply do not have these prerequisites. Before they are ready to make good use of technology, they must make substantial investments in education. As economists would say, there must be complementarity between physical capital (that is, capital in plant, equipment, machinery, etc.) and human capital, which is the amount invested in education—not alone formal education in schools and colleges but also informal education in on-the-job training, in apprenticeship programs, and in all the variety of other ways by which people may be trained to make better use of their abilities.

In the triad of features that make an efficient society, the last is economic organization. Any nation's economy may be organized in either of two general patterns: as a price system, organized around a market economy, or as a planning system. In the planning system, a central authority decides how much is to be produced, what prices shall be paid for it, how much labor and how much capital work at it, and all similar determinants. This, of course, has not been the American experience. Rather, our economy demonstrates the way in which a market economy works and, indeed, the way in which a market economy has been phenomenally successful in organizing a society to produce high living standards. It is a market economy, then, that will be examined here.

No one tells a market economy what to do. Instead, it follows Adam Smith's old dictum that man's self-interest will guide him to produce the right amount and that competition will see not only that it gets produced, but that labor and capital move to the right kinds of industry because that will be where their participation is most profitable. One important detail is needed to make this system work: it takes motivation. People must be motivated to raise their standards of living. If this occurs, and if we have competition, then people will move to jobs where they can get higher wages; capital will go where the highest rate of return exists; businessmen will organize themselves to produce the things that are in growing demand and to sell their products where prices are such that they can make profits. In essence, this is the way a market economy works if it works at all. Ever since early Colonial times, America has been a society in which people have been motivated to earn maximum gains for themselves, so its market economy has worked efficiently.

The ultimate determinant of what is produced, therefore, has been the consumer, who has decided, by what he is willing to buy, how much is to be produced of what goods. While nobody tells anybody directly what to do and how to do it, it turns out that this market economy produces the kinds of goods and services that are needed to make it workable. What are the specific requirements for this self-regulating system to function?

In product markets—that is, in the production of goods and services—competition is needed first, because it forces producers to attract customers by means of lower prices and better quality. Also needed are markets big enough to utilize all the inherent efficiency in the latest technology.

In addition to the product market, there is need in this type of economy for efficient factor markets—that is, for providing an adequate supply of factors such as land, labor, capital, and managerial talents. Factor markets must also be responsive to profitable opportunities in just the way described for product markets. They also must be competitive to such a degree that, again, efficiency will be assured in the movement of these factors to provide maximum output. Government has a role in such an economy, but it is the restricted one of doing only those things that the market cannot perform effectively for itself. This controversial question of what constitutes the government's role will be discussed later in some detail. At this point, it is enough to point out that it does have a part to play.

This very brief exposition of sources of economic growth slights a number of major issues. Improvement in the factor markets, for example, means among other things that the capital market is developed; but nothing has been said about either the volume of savings (which in a market economy reflects individuals' decisions to consume or to save) or about the role of investment in economic growth. The latter is a subject that will be examined further in subsequent chapters, but here we may point out that capital plays a role in economic growth through (1) increasing the stock of tools, machinery, equipment, land improvements, etc., with which man works to produce goods; (2) providing funds to purchase raw materials, hire labor, etc., before income is received from the resultant output; (3) improving the quality of the labor force (investment in human capital); (4) increasing the stock of knowledge that underlies technological change; (5) embodying this new knowledge in machines and equipment. It has been established that increases in capital inputs as traditionally defined—that is, numbers 1 and 2 above —account for only a very small fraction of recorded productivity change in the United States. This is a very important finding, because it casts doubt on the traditional view that simply a rise in the rate of capital formation (as traditionally defined) is the critical factor. Rather, it appears that it is capital embodying productivity increases (broadly conceived) that is most important.

A summary of this brief discussion of economic growth may serve to pull it together. Increased output from a given amount of inputs of labor, capital, land, and managerial talent constitutes increased efficiency. This can come about from better machines and tools (as embodied in new capital equipment), better educated and trained labor (human capital investment), improvements in the organization of markets. It can also come about from people shifting from poor land to better land or from their being employed in activities in which efficiency is higher than in their former pursuit (such as shifting from agriculture to manufacturing in the nineteenth century). All of these sources of improving productivity have been important in America's past and will come in for more attention in later chapters.

It is important to distinguish carefully between the economics of growth and that of full employment. The former is concerned with the growing efficiency of an economy, the latter with the degree to which the resources, capital, and manpower of a society are fully utilized. Although the economics of growth has dominated the foregoing analysis, the extent to which resources are employed is also obviously important to the over-all welfare of a society. Unemployed resources represent unused capacity, which means not only lower income than the society is capable of attaining, but also, for labor in particular, it means unemployed workers with all the attendant hardships and distress of such involuntary unemployment. Our history has been characterized by recurring periods of unemployment. They are endemic to a market economy where the level of economic activity is the sum of the individual decisions of entrepreneurs and consumers. The degree to which we mitigate the inevitable fluctuations in income and minimize the lapses from full employment depends upon the efficiency of the banking system and the monetary and fiscal policies of the federal government. An efficient banking system not only makes the capital market work smoothly (channeling savings into investment) but will also affect the supply of money, which is one of the major influences upon fluctuation in income.[6] The fiscal and monetary policies of the federal government influence how much people will spend and therefore can significantly modify fluctuations, but it is only in the past two decades that fiscal and monetary policies of our federal government have been consistently directed toward a policy of full employment (Chapter 14).

A discussion of unemployment leads directly to the second of the two major concerns of the economic historian. This is the aspect of welfare—literally, how well did any group fare in its economic setting? In over-all terms, the welfare of all groups is reflected in the distribution of income in the society, and changes in this income distribution will mirror shifts in the relative well-being of different groups. Many of the major issues that confront the economic historian concern the real or alleged improvement or deterioration in the income position of a segment of the society. The standard of life of the worker during the industrial revolution, the discontent of the farmer in the late nineteenth century, or the antipoverty campaign in modern times are a small sample of such issues. Accurate quantitative data are necessary to measure the actual change in income status of any group, and economic analysis will provide an explanation.

[6] A major issue of economic theory of the past decade has been the importance of the money supply as a determinant of economic activity. That the two sides are not really as far apart as the noise of the controversy would suggest is made clear in a recent monumental study by Milton Friedman and Anna Schwartz, *A Monetary History of the United States, 1867-1960* (Princeton, N.J.: Princeton Univ., 1963), and in reviews by leading critics of the monetary school. Especially see James Tobin, "The Monetary Interpretation of History," *AER*, LV, No. 3 (June 1965), 464-85.

NOTE: *AER*, the abbreviation for *American Economic Review* is typical of abbreviations used throughout the footnotes and source lines for tables and charts. A complete list with full titles appears on p. viii.

III

Explanation of issues of welfare and growth, therefore, comes from economic analysis, and these explanations are tested by determining the extent to which they provide a "best fit" to the available evidence. Sometimes when issues of welfare and growth are raised, they can be directly resolved by accurate and precise measurements. For example, it is commonly asserted that the more rapid fall of farm prices, compared to the prices of other goods in the last third of the nineteenth century, was one of the causes of agrarian discontent. Another common assertion is that the Civil War accelerated economic growth of the United States and made possible its industrialization.

The role of farm prices in agrarian discontent can be ascertained by getting good price indices of agricultural and other commodities during this period. Surprisingly, the results show that agricultural prices fell no more rapidly than other prices. The second assertion can be examined critically by getting data on the rate of growth of the American economy and on the growth of manufacturing output. These show that the rate of growth of the economy was highest in the decades before and after the Civil War, but very slow in the war decade. Manufacturing output had already been growing very rapidly before the war; and indeed, by any standards we were already a great industrial nation. Therefore, neither assertion will withstand the test of examination in the light of readily available statistics.

A more common assertion that defies simple statistical testing, however, is that the society or the groups were better off or worse off than they would have been had "circumstances" been different. In subsequent chapters, we shall examine the following familiar statements about the welfare of groups, or the American society as a whole, in American history.

> British policy was vindictive and injurious to the Colonial economy after 1763.

> The railroad was indispensable for American economic growth.

> Speculators and railroads (through land grants) monopolized the best western lands in the nineteenth century and slowed down the westward movement.

In the era of the robber barons, farmers and workers were exploited.

In each case the statement is really incomplete. If we are to make any accurate appraisals of the issues and of the welfare implications, they should read more properly as follows.

British policies were restrictive and injurious to the Colonial economy after 1763, compared to what would have taken place had the Colonies been independent during these years; or more precisely, income of the Colonies under British rule after 1763 was less than it would have been had the Colonists been free and independent.

Income in the United States would have been significantly less had there been no railroads.

A different (but specified) land policy would have led to more rapid westward settlement in the nineteenth century.

In the absence of the monopolistic practices of the robber barons, farm income and real wages would have been significantly higher.

There are three essential ingredients in this analysis. First, the alternative being hypothecated must be "reasonable." Thus, in the case of Colonial income, it would not make sense to hypothecate a world of free trade as the alternative against which to measure income, since that was simply not the likely alternative in the world of 1763-1775. Second, to construct the hypothetical alternative requires economic analysis, in order to make sense about how an economy would have operated under different conditions. This is impossible without understanding the way in which an economy does operate and without the use of economic theory. Third, good statistical data are necessary to measure what actual income was, compared to the hypothetical income to be developed in the hypothetical alternative. I do not mean to suggest that this method resolves all problems in measuring relative welfare of people in our past. We may disagree about what is a reasonable alternative. We may even argue about the quality of the economic analysis used in creating the hypothetical alternative. And finally, we may not have the statistical data to measure accurately what the difference was.

At numerous points in successive chapters, it will be necessary to stop short of answering the questions that are raised because the necessary statistical data have not yet been developed. But this is the method that must be employed if we are to resolve the innumerable controversies about welfare in our past and to make more meaningful statements about what happened to diverse groups and to the society as a whole in the course of American economic development.[7]

One additional point should be stressed. What actually happened to people, and what people thought happened, were frequently not the same thing. For example, with hindsight it may turn out that the American Colonists fared rather well under English rule and, indeed, that they would not have fared as well under alternative possibilities. But the Colonists acted upon the view that they would be better off under a different set of circumstances, therefore fought a Revolution, became independent, and changed American history.[8] The actions they pursued were predicated on the views, right or wrong, that they held at that time. Thus, throughout economic history, we are as interested in trying to understand what people thought was happening to them as we are in trying to arrive at an accurate assessment of what actually did happen.[9] Now let us turn and look at an over-all picture of our economic development.

[7] There is nothing novel about the use of the hypothetical alternative. The welfare statements cited above are all paraphrases of familiar statements made by historians, and historical writings are replete with similar assertions. The novelty is in turning such assertions into testable propositions, and this necessarily involves the methods described above. The concept of counterfactual propositions (hypothetical alternatives) was originally examined in economic history in a pathbreaking article by John R. Meyer and Alfred H. Conrad, "Economic Theory, Statistical Inference and Economic History," *JEH*, XVII (Dec. 1957). In the literature of philosophy of science, counterfactual propositions have been extensively examined. See Nelson Goodman, "The Problem of Counterfactual Conditions," *JP*, XLIV (Feb. 1947), and R.B. Braithwaite, *Scientific Explanation* (New York: Harper, 1960), pp. 295-318.

[8] If this should be the case, there are two possible explanatory hypotheses: (1) that they were misguided in their economic assessment, or (2) perhaps more plausibly, that they were primarily motivated by other than economic issues.

[9] Since traditional textbooks in history usually carry a full account of what people thought was happening to them, this subject has been slighted in this very brief study except where it necessarily emerges in specific welfare issues, as in chapters 11 and 12.

chapter 2

AN OVERVIEW
OF THE DEVELOPMENT
OF THE U.S. ECONOMY

Before examining specific issues of growth and welfare, we need an overview of the growth and structural changes of the past three and one-half centuries. The topography of this economic landscape can be seen in the following tables and charts drawn from the accumulation of statistical data. They are supplemented at many points by the rich accumulation of qualitative information gathered from the literature of economic history.

Since the earliest national income estimate of 1840, the economy has grown at a rate of about 1.6 per cent per year in real terms (Chart 1). This means that in terms of constant prices, the average per capita income has risen by that figure, and this is roughly analogous to what has actually happened to the average standard of life or the average well-being of people, although it is well to remember the caution in the first chapter that there are real limitations to using per capita income figures and drawing too neat a pattern from them. At first glance, the figure of 1.6 per cent may not sound like a very impressive annual growth rate; but it turns out to have quite spectacular compound results. It means that every 43 years, income per capita, in constant prices, has doubled in America. In today's prices, average income per head is around $2,400, whereas back in 1840, when measurements began, it was $400 in today's

CHART 1.   PER CAPITA INCOME, 1840-1940

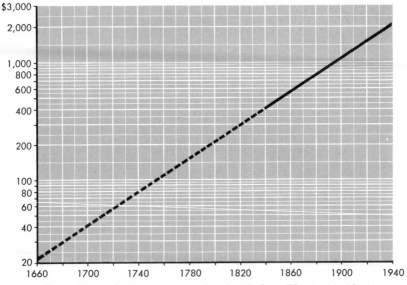

Source: Raymond Goldsmith, testimony before the U.S. Cong. JEC, printed in "Employment, Growth, and the Price Level," 86th Cong., 1st Sess., Part II, 1959. (Washington: GPO, 1959), pp. 277-78.

prices. This raises the question, what happened before 1840? We lack information on income before that date. Less is known about the economy, and the statistics are still far from adequate. It is probable, however, that per capita real income grew at a slower pace.

Chart 1 illustrates why the growth rate of 1.6 per cent per year probably did not exist much earlier than 1840. Projected back before that date, the same growth rate very rapidly reaches unreasonably low levels of per capita income. The extended line would indicate that, in today's dollars, per capita annual income would have been $145 in 1776; $80 in 1740, and $30 in 1680. Since the early Americans did not starve, these are ridiculous figures, having no real significance. It therefore appears likely that the rate of growth of the economy must have been slower in the period before 1840 (although when the change takes place, we don't know). This point has some significance for later analysis.

What were some of the salient features of the Colonial economy? First of all, most people worked on the land, and this was the
main source of economic activity; a preponderant 90 per cent of the
population engaged in farming or in pursuits directly related to
farming. There was little increase in the efficiency of farming in the
Colonial period, and therefore little growth in per capita income
resulting from productivity gains in agriculture. It is to be expected
that some improvements in efficiency did occur with increases in
the size of the market and with better marketing methods; but
there was comparatively little shift to better land during this period,
and it is doubtful that living standards rose rapidly.

Meanwhile, really substantial gains in efficiency were taking
place in another part of our economy that was another main source
of income—international shipping. In Colonial times, America was
already a major shipping power, engaging in fishing, whaling, and
particularly in carrying the goods of the world—not only from our
own shores to other nations, but between foreign countries. Colonial efficiency in shipping improved substantially during that period
and became an important feature of the total economy. A good
share of credit for the increased efficiency goes to an event seldom
thought of today—the decline in piracy. As freebooters were driven
from the seas, fewer men and guns were needed for protection on
ships, and this turned out to be an important source of lowering the
real cost of ocean transportation.

In Colonial times there was little manufacturing. Shipbuilding
was an important activity, and there were some small-scale manufacturing activities like making iron. By and large, however, it was
a farming, shipping, and commercial society, not heavily involved
in manufacturing. Since America of that day was a small market
with relatively expensive labor, it is not surprising that the English
provided most of our manufacturing.

In terms of the determinants of economic growth discussed in
Chapter 1, one would expect to find that the Colonial economy
improved only gradually and probably not at the 1.6 per cent per
year figure cited for more recent times. There was little technological change in agriculture, the major source of income. And
improvements that were occurring in economic organization were
still very gradual, in the forms of increasing efficiency in shipping,

of larger markets, of the beginnings of towns, and of better communication and transportation. It is doubtful, therefore, that the Colonial economy could have been expected to grow as strikingly, over-all, as it did after 1840.

What about the *extensive* growth of the Colonial period? Rapid population growth certainly characterized the period. A glance at Chart 2 gives an approximation of the course of Colonial population, increasing from negligible numbers up to 331,000 by

CHART 2. ESTIMATED POPULATION OF AMERICAN COLONIES, 1610-1780
(In 1,000's)

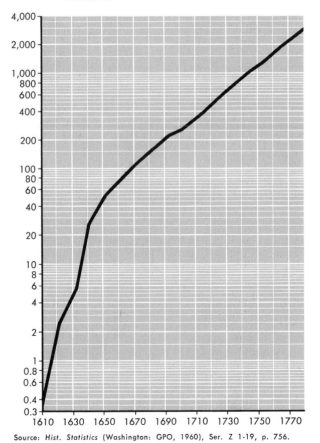

Source: *Hist. Statistics* (Washington: GPO, 1960), Ser. Z 1-19, p. 756.

1710, then soaring to more than 2,000,000 at the time of the Revolutionary War. Immigrants made up much of this increase. Many came voluntarily, free and clear; others put themselves into indenture, agreeing to work for someone for a prescribed period in return for payment of their passage and for specified benefits at the end of the indenture. Still others, in substantial numbers, were brought in as slaves who provided a great share of the labor force in the southern colonies. Extensive growth in the Colonial period, therefore, consisted of a notable increase of population; settlements along the coasts, a gradual movement into the interior, and the beginning of an economy based upon agriculture and shipping, which will be examined further on in more detail.

Colonial days were turbulent. The settlers frequently had grievances against the British, against the French and Spanish on their borders, against the Indians along the frontier, and at times against each other. These disputes reflected the Colonists' views that their welfare was being adversely affected, and at times they led to open warfare. The actual income effects of these controversies have not been measured. The most significant for American history

TABLE 2. **VALUE OF OUTPUT BY INDUSTRY IN CURRENT PRICES,**
1839-1899 (In billions of dollars)

Year	Total	Agriculture	Mining	Manufacturing	Construction
1839	$ 1.04	$0.71	$0.01	$0.24	$0.08
1844	1.09	0.69	0.01	0.31	0.08
1849	1.40	0.83	0.02	0.45	0.11
1854	2.39	1.46	0.03	0.66	0.23
1859	2.57	1.50	0.03	0.82	0.23
1869	4.83	2.54	0.13	1.63	0.54
1874	5.40	2.53	0.15	2.07	0.65
1879	5.30	2.60	0.15	1.96	0.59
1884	7.09	2.84	0.20	3.05	1.01
1889	7.87	2.77	0.28	3.73	1.10
1894	7.83	2.64	0.29	3.60	1.30
1899	10.20	3.40	0.47	5.04	1.29

Source: *Hist. Statistics*, Ser. F 10-21, p. 139.

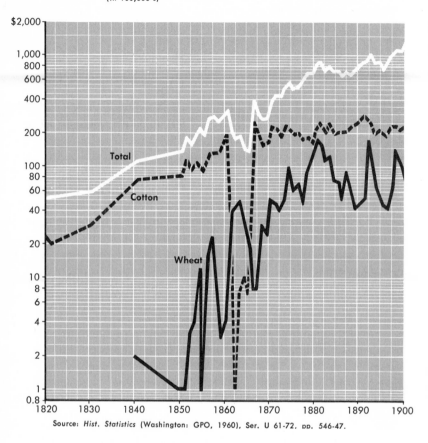

Source: *Hist. Statistics* (Washington: GPO, 1960), Ser. U 61-72. pp. 546-47.

were the issues between the Crown and the Colonists from 1763 to 1775, which are examined in the following chapter.

Turning now to the nineteenth century (beginning, however, with the first census, which was in 1790), we may take a sweeping look at the pattern of that century's economy. Table 2 points up the predominant role of agriculture. In 1839, when accurate figures were first obtained, agriculture accounted for 70 per cent of the value of commodity output of the economy and certain agricultural commodities were particularly important. Of these, cotton played a dominant early role and was a large part of total exports. As Chart 3 shows, cotton comprised more than half of American exports in the years before the Civil War. After the war, it continued as an important part of the agricultural economy, although the value of wheat exports became a significant and growing challenger.

Agriculture expanded with the opening up and settlement of the West. It is not surprising, therefore, that as new, rich lands were developed, the agricultural output continually expanded and the kinds of agriculture became diversified. A second look at Table 2 shows another noteworthy development. Although agriculture grew all through the century in absolute terms of value of output,

CHART 4. **AGRICULTURAL AND NONAGRICULTURAL LABOR FORCE,
1820-1940**
(In 100,000's)

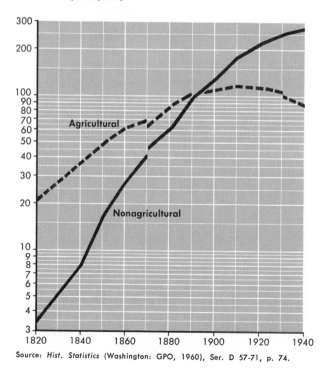

Source: *Hist. Statistics* (Washington: GPO, 1960), Ser. D 57-71, p. 74.

CHART 5. **POPULATION IN URBAN AND RURAL TERRITORY,**
BY SIZE OF PLACE, 1790-1950
(In 100,000's)

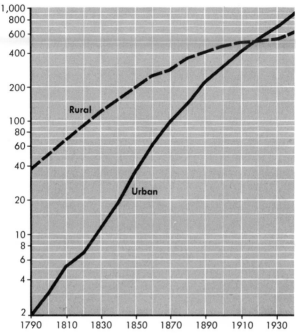

Source: *Hist. Statistics* (Washington: GPO, 1960), Ser. A 195-209, p. 14.

relatively, it declined. Whereas it was 70 per cent of commodity output in 1839, it was only 33 per cent of output by the end of that century. Different statistics illustrate the same point in Chart 4, which shows the composition of the labor force during the century. How were people employed? The earliest available figures, in 1820, show 2 million out of 2.8 million people working on the land; other aspects of the economy were relatively negligible. But as the century moved forward, the change in the employment pattern is striking. It is true that the number of agricultural workers increased; but growing much more rapidly were the tallies of those working in manufacturing, construction, transportation, and trade. Later in the century, proportionately more and more were working in activities other than agriculture; as a matter of fact, 1910 was a peak year in absolute terms for agricultural workers, whose total has been declining ever since that date. The distribution of the labor force mirrors strikingly that while we were a rapidly growing agricultural economy, other sectors, particularly manufacturing, were growing even more rapidly. By 1880, only one half of our people were working in agriculture.

Now if people shift from agriculture to other activities, comparable shifts are expected in how they live. Logically, they will move off the farms to the cities, and that is exactly what shows up in Chart 5. Classing "urban" population as those living in communities of 2,500 or more, and "rural" as communities of less than that number, the distribution is continually moving in the direction of an increasingly urban society. By the twentieth century, America

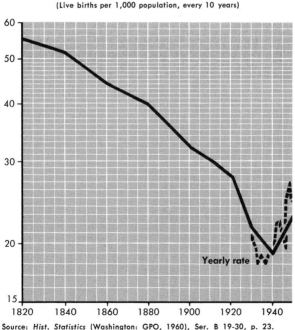

CHART 6. BIRTH RATE, 1820-1950
(Live births per 1,000 population, every 10 years)

Source: *Hist. Statistics* (Washington: GPO, 1960), Ser. B 19-30, p. 23.

was becoming predominantly urban, but not until 1920 did urban territory include more people than rural territory. The whole process of westward movement and shift from farm to city is tied to where people worked and the kinds of jobs they had. A sidelight to this pattern of rural-urban relationship is shown in Chart 6, which shows the domestic birth rate in America. The decline from 55 per thousand in 1820 to 18.4 per thousand in 1936 appears to be related to the shift of people from the farm to the city. Demographers have speculated that children are not only a greater asset on the farm but are less costly for the farmer than for the city dweller to bring up; so that as people became more urbanized, their families grew smaller. In modern times, this pattern tends to be reversed in urban areas, and there has been an increase in birth rates, but this phenomenon is observable only in very recent times.

An integral part of nineteenth century expansion was the growth of our banking system, of wholesale and retail marketing organization, and a more efficient transportation network. All contributed significantly to productivity increase by lowering the real costs of credit and of handling and moving goods.

The high cost of carrying bulk goods in Colonial times limited commercial production to areas adjacent to navigable waterways. Improved roads and then turnpikes after the Revolutionary War widened local markets, but the major improvements in internal transportation came with the growth of water transport on the Mississippi River system (particularly with the innovation of the steamboat for upriver carriage of goods in 1816) and the growth of a canal system connecting the Great Lakes with both the Mississippi system and with the eastern seaboard. The development of the railroad after 1830, in turn, displaced the canal and dominated internal transport history during the rest of the nineteenth century (Chapter 9).

The orientation of the Colonies toward external markets (and the purchase of goods from abroad) led to rather well-developed merchant houses dealing in exports and imports; however, as internal trade and commerce grew, institutions to move goods from producers to consumers also grew and necessarily became more complex. The evolution from the itinerant peddler, jobber, roving merchant, and general store (often associated with a local factory) to specialized wholesale houses and equally specialized retail outlets was a nineteenth century development, and it is mirrored in the growing percentage of the labor force engaged in trade, increasing from about 6 per cent in 1850 to more than 10 per cent by the turn of the century.

Banking was in its infancy the decade after Independence was achieved. The first chartered bank was established in 1784, but banking growth was slow in early years. The establishment of the First United States Bank in 1791 provided an important impetus for tying together government fiscal activities with the early banking community. Although the bank was an important step in the growth of the capital market, it engendered considerable opposition, and its charter was not renewed after its initial twenty-year term. Five years later, however, in 1816, the Second United States Bank was chartered. After a rocky start under undistinguished leadership it became, under Nicholas Biddle, a major influence in regulating the commercial banks, in acting as a reserve bank when banks needed additional specie, and in integrating the banking system. In short, it anticipated in many respects the role expected of a modern central bank in influencing the money supply and tying together federal government fiscal activities with the banking system. It became an even more controversial institution than its predecessor and a central issue in the election of 1832. When Andrew Jackson triumphed, the bank's fate was settled; and with the expiration of its charter, central banking was not again to be revived until the next century.

The demise of the second bank resulted in a mounting number of banks, each issuing its own notes. By 1860 there were 1500 banks individually issuing, on the average, six different types of notes. Moreover, the worth of the notes varied strikingly—some were "as good as gold," others were the worthless paper of broken banks. The Civil War and growing pressure for a national banking system led to the passage in 1864 of the National Banking Act, which permitted federal charter of banks and required that such banks keep reserves in cash or as deposits with a national bank in one of seventeen large cities. Similarly, banks in these large cities had the same option to keep part of their reserves in New York City banks. The result was the beginning of a nationwide banking system. A central

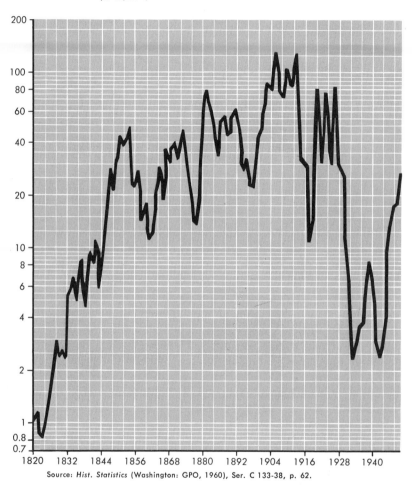

CHART 7.   IMMIGRATION, 1820-1950
(In 10,000's)

Source: *Hist. Statistics* (Washington: GPO, 1960), Ser. C 133-38, p. 62.

CHART 8. FOREIGN INVESTMENT IN U.S. (NET LIABILITIES), 1789-1900

(In millions of dollars)

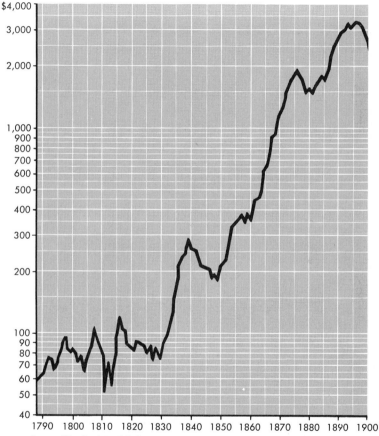

Source: *Hist. Statistics* (Washington: GPO, 1960), Ser. U 207, p. 566.

TABLE 3.   UNITED STATES PERCENTAGE OF
WORLD MANUFACTURING OUTPUT (World = 100 per cent)

Period	U.S.A.	United Kingdom	Germany	France	Russia	Others
1870	23.3	31.8	13.2	10.3	3.7	17.7
1881-1885	28.6	26.6	13.9	8.6	3.4	18.9
1896-1900	30.1	19.5	16.6	7.1	5.0	21.7
1906-1910	35.3	14.7	15.9	6.4	5.0	22.7
1913	35.8	14.0	15.7	6.4	5.5	22.6
1926-1929	42.2	9.4	11.6	6.6	4.3	25.9

Source: League of Nations, *Industrialization and Foreign Trade*, Geneva, 1945, p. 13.

banking system to unite federal government fiscal policy with the banking system did not occur, however, until the creation of the Federal Reserve System in 1914.

One more aspect, important to the economy in the nineteenth century (and particularly in its first half) was our relationship with the rest of the world. We were yet a small part of the great world, and the fact that foreigners wanted our goods and services contributed significantly to our extensive expansion. Cotton and shipping have already been discussed. But foreigners also wanted other kinds of goods—agricultural products in the early part of the nineteenth century and then, as the century wore on and we became an industrial nation, our manufactured goods as well.

Perhaps more important than the role of trade in the country's growth was immigration, and Chart 7 pictures this immensely significant aspect of our over-all development. Beginning in the 1840's with the Irish famine and its consequences, vast numbers of people turned to America in a tide that flowed through the decades until World War I. This was a swelling movement of unprecedented numbers willing to take their chances in a New World. Undoubtedly, it was one of the important formative aspects of our expansion.

Foreigners also invested heavily in the new nation, as illustrated in Chart 8. This was particularly true of the British who, having confidence in America's future, invested in canals, railroads, and cotton plantations. Although foreign investment was significant, it probably has been overstressed in the history of national development. Foreign capital was important in the 1830's, but thereafter its proportion of total capital formation dwindled, even though the absolute amount grew substantially.

Over-all, the international economy contributed through investment; it contributed through people; and it contributed through trading goods that could be produced more efficiently elsewhere in exchange for those that we could produce relatively efficiently. It also contributed in one essential way that cannot be shown in graphic form—ideas. The technology America borrowed in the

CHART 9.   **COMMODITY OUTPUT IN FIVE-YEAR AVERAGES, 1839-1899**
(In billions of dollars)

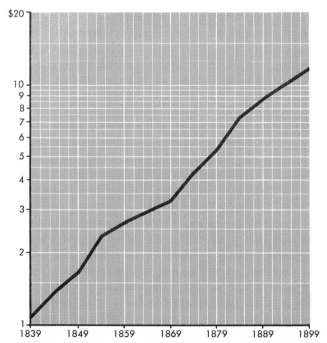

Source: Robert E. Gallman, "The United States Commodity Output, 1839-1899," *Trends in the American Economy in the Nineteenth Century,* a report of the NBER (Princeton, N.J.: Princeton Univ., 1960), pp. 16, 43.

nineteenth century, basically from Europe and particularly from Great Britain, was a major source of improvement in productivity.

By 1860 the United States had become a major industrial nation, second only to Britain. Chart 9 shows the decade rate of

TABLE 4. POPULATION REDISTRIBUTION
(Per cent of total)

Region	1870	1880	1890	1900
New England	8.8	8.0	7.5	7.4
Middle Atlantic	24.7	23.4	22.5	22.5
Great Lakes	22.9	22.3	21.4	21.0
Southeast	29.1	27.3	25.5	25.1
Plains	9.7	12.3	14.2	13.6
Southwest	2.5	3.5	4.4	5.5
Mountain	0.4	0.9	1.4	1.7
Far West	1.8	2.3	3.1	3.2
U.S. total	39,818,449	50,155,783	62,947,714	75,994,575

Source: Original from 17th U.S. Census, 1950, as contained in Harvey S. Perloff, et al.,

growth in manufacturing output. The progress of America into first place among industrial nations may be seen in Table 3, where the percentages of world manufacturing output are shown from 1870 to 1929. From 23 per cent in 1870, the nation's share rose to more than 40 per cent of the world's manufacturing output by 1926-1929. Between the Civil War and World War I, an already thriving manufacturing enormously expanded.

At the same time, population was redistributing itself around the United States. In the early days, of course, all settlement was along the coastal line; by 1860, the population was moving out across the Appalachian Mountains into the Great Lakes area, the middle Atlantic area, and into the cotton-producing South. The Gold Rush of 1848 pushed the frontiers of population westward to California and Oregon. After the Civil War, the movement was primarily across the Mississippi into the rich area of the plains, that whole vast area from the Mississippi to the Rocky Mountains, which became peopled and settled during that period. Population expanded from New England, the oldest area, into the Midwest and then into the Far West. This particular pattern, taking place all through that period, is mirrored in Table 4, as it occurred from 1870 on. Not only were people relocating, but they were continu-

1910	1920	1930	1940	1950
7.1	7.0	6.7	6.4	6.2
23.0	23.1	23.3	23.0	22.3
19.8	20.3	20.6	20.2	20.2
23.9	23.0	22.2	22.9	22.4
12.7	11.9	10.8	10.8	9.3
6.6	7.0	7.4	7.4	7.6
2.2	2.4	2.2	2.3	2.3
4.7	5.3	6.8	7.5	9.7
91,972,266	105,710,620	122,775,046	131,669,275	150,697,361

Regions, Resources, and Economic Growth (Baltimore: Johns Hopkins, 1960), pp. 124, 225.

ally moving into new and rich agricultural lands. At the same time that America rose to first place among manufacturing nations of the world, it also became the world's leading agricultural nation. In short, America became a supplier to the world both of industrial products and of greatly increased output of agricultural products.

The nineteenth century, therefore, was marked not only by an unprecedented increase in people, capital, and land—spurring its extensive growth—but also by increasing efficiency of these production factors, resulting in intensive growth. The most noteworthy aspects were (1) adoption of the most efficient techniques in the world in manufacturing and in agriculture; (2) significant increase in education in America, making possible the use of the latest technology and a new efficiency stemming from substantial research both in industry and in agriculture; and (3) availability of a vast new United States market of unprecedented size, which made feasible all the efficiency of large-scale production.

If over-all growth characterized this period, so did frequently recurring economic distress and hardship for diverse groups. The most important sources of such distress were the recurrent depressions and recessions of the nineteenth century; 1819, 1837, 1839, 1857, 1873, and 1893 were all years that marked the onset of falling income and increasing unemployment of varying degrees of severity. There are not accurate statistics to measure the fall in income or the amount of unemployment during these periods. As an increasing percentage of the population shifted from self-sufficient agriculture to production for the market, the impact of these depressions became greater, since they affected more and more people. There is no evidence that the depressions themselves became more severe, however (in fact, probably the depression of 1839 was the most severe of the century).

The immigrant or the farm boy who left the farm was likely to seek employment in the new factory towns as manufacturing grew. His hours were long and the conditions onerous by present standards. Factory towns were frequently unsanitary, overlaid with coal dust, and housing conditions were grim. Although it is doubtful that the new factory worker's real income fell (Chapter 5), he bore the serious costs of monotonous discipline during long hours at a machine and the insecurity of employment as workers were let out during depressions.

The farmer's well-being, too, was becoming more dependent upon the market. On top of drought, locusts, and other natural disasters, wide fluctuations in prices received for crops made his income subject to broad swings (Chapter 11). His lot improved in the nineteenth century, but this undeniable statement hides the diversity of economic experience that held disaster in the short run for many.

It is not surprising, therefore, that the nineteenth century was characterized by a variety of protest movements against working conditions, job insecurity, low prices, and monopoly.

Utopian schemes and programs of reform were continually advanced as solutions to these problems. Trade-union membership was never a significant percentage of the labor force until well into the twentieth century. Attempts to form a nationwide labor organization such as the National Labor Union in 1866 and the Knights of Labor (which had its major expansion in the 1870's and early

Eighties) turned out to be temporary, and it was not until the founding of the American Federation of Labor in 1881 that trade unions achieved permanent organization on a national basis. Farm protest movements had a larger impact upon public policy. Between the Civil War and 1900, the Greenback, Granger, and Populist movements attempted to increase prices and to undertake basic economic reforms in the expectation that they would raise farm real income (Chapter 11).

A growing source of concern to worker and farmer alike was the development of the trust and of other forms of organization having significant monopoly power. The publication of Henry Demarest Lloyd's *Wealth Against Commonwealth* and Ida Tarbell's *History of the Standard Oil Company* provided early examples of the growing literature of reformers and "muckrakers" protesting against the growth of monopoly. The reformers not only pointed up the dangers of the trust but exposed political graft and corruption and made Americans aware of the importance of conserving and setting aside the rich natural-resource heritage of forests and scenic attractions in the face of the onrushing extensive expansion of the economy.

World War I marks the end of an era, a boundary beyond which nations became more self-contained. America dammed the stream of immigration, and other countries erected tariff barriers, as we had done earlier. An international economy in which people, capital, and ideas had enjoyed free interchanges for a century became hampered by restrictions on the movement of people and by restrictions on trade. World War I also marked the end of a relatively peaceful century and the beginning of a century marked by global war and a global depression. The decade of the Twenties was prosperous, but the 1929 crash and subsequent decade of depression resulted in a greater fall in income and a more cataclysmic economic period than any ever experienced before. It had long-run implications for our future views about how to cope with comparable situations and about the policies to be pursued. The depression of the Thirties continued in some measure until our 1941 entry into World War II and the resultant explosive expansion to meet war needs.

In taking this overview of what happened in the twentieth

century—a notable growth of the economy interrupted by the Great Depression but continued thereafter—a few salient changes should be recognized. One was the development of new products. The twentieth century introduced the automobile, the electric refrigerator, and all the other comforts known as durable consumer goods; and it inspired a vast concern with services as compared with goods. The result was a significant change in the employment pattern and in the structure of the economy to meet these new demands of a prospering people.[1] A second change was a turnabout in America's international role: instead of being a debtor nation, as at the turn of the century, it became a creditor; and since World War II, it has expended vast sums attempting to promote and assist the development of the rest of the world. No longer is America "just another nation," but a dominant nation viewing itself as having a responsibility to other countries in the world. And a third transformation was one that took place in the role of government in the American economy. When the federal government first emerged in 1790, it spent but a tiny fraction of national income and was involved in relatively few concerns. Contrast the role of government in the American economy today! The federal government alone (forgetting for the moment state and local governments) has an annual budget in the neighborhood of $100 billion. Government at all levels expends somewhere around a quarter of total national income. Obviously, government now has a role different from any it has ever had before—one of vastly more scope in regulating and ordering the working of our economy.

This brief sketch of American economic experience will serve as a backdrop for an analytical explanation of specific issues of growth and welfare. We begin with Colonial America.

---

[1] Between 1919 and 1957, while nonagricultural employment doubled, employment in services tripled. *Hist. Statistics* (Washington: GPO, 1960), p. 73.

chapter 3

THE COLONIAL ECONOMY

Colonial settlement was a direct outgrowth of the expansion of western Europe in the fifteenth, sixteenth, and seventeenth centuries. The Western world was emerging from a relatively self-sufficient feudal society in which people produced most of their own goods, raised their own food, made their own clothing and equipment. It had been a world in which trade and commerce played a relatively minor role, a world characterized in western Europe by the self-contained economy of the manor house and the small village which the manor house dominated. Now this picture was changing. Independent manorial lords were being coalesced into larger nation states. More important, the ideological climate was changing. There was radical ferment in religious views and articulate concern about political problems and political philosophy. Science was beginning to emerge with a quickening interest in physics, chemistry, and fundamental mathematics. Evolving, too, was economic organization, the growth out of self-sufficiency to a market economy. As trade and commerce increased, factor markets improved in efficiency. Labor became more mobile, either as a result of release from the feudal obligations of serfdom or as workers were driven off by enclosures of land (although recent research suggests that this was a less important influence than had been heretofore believed). There gradually evolved groups of savers and of borrowers of funds, as well as ways to get the savings into investments by organized channels as a capital market developed. Factor markets were developing those conditions that make a market economy possible.

Product markets were also improving. With the growth of commerce, a need appeared for new companies to produce goods for trade with other parts of the world. Monopoly characterized much of this early development, but it tended to disappear in the face of effective competition—if not within a country, then of competition posed by other countries in the course of exchange of goods. So began what is called mercantilism—a world in which government policy and economic activity combined to affect in many ways the direction of the evolving nations. One implicit assumption in this mercantilist world was significant for the whole pattern of development. Most participants in the mercantilist world considered that the way to get greater wealth was to take it from someone else. Implicitly, they assumed that only one pie, of fixed size, was produced in the world and that they could have a bigger serving only by helping themselves to their neighbor's slice. This basic assumption of static productivity helps explain the efforts of the mercantilist nations to devise schemes that would expand their wealth at the expense of other countries. Was the assumption true in its time? Since population increased greatly from the year 1000 to 1700 (which necessarily led to the cultivation of poorer land) and average income appears to have remained fairly steady, the total pie must have increased substantially—not only as a result of increasing amounts of factors of production but as a result of growing efficiency as well. Looking at that earlier world in terms of the determinants of productivity discussed in Chapter 1, it appears that increasing technological change was already in evidence. Indeed, many innovations had already come about in the several centuries before what is definitively called the Industrial Revolution, not only in early manufacturing but in improving the efficiency of agriculture as well.

In addition, human resources were developing with the spread of writing and reading, and particularly with the advent of printing, so that probably education and knowledge were becoming more widely disseminated; this certainly was a factor in improving efficiency. Still another and the largest source of such improvement was the development of the factor and product markets, already discussed, together with economies of scale that came from the expansion of trade and commerce and from the resultant specialization and division of labor.[1] In short, while the first two determinants may have been fairly important, it is probable that improving economic organization turned out to be a particularly crucial aspect of the way in which this market world was developing. As a pivot for the whole growth of commerce and trade, shipping gives us a case in point. By 1600 the Dutch had already developed a ship called the flute, as efficient as any ship to be developed for several centuries thereafter. Increases in productivity after that date came largely from greater efficiency of use (such as the fact that fewer crew members were needed because of the decline of piracy), from the development of larger ships to match the increasing size of shipments and cargoes, and from declining time that ships were idle in port—all aspects of improving economic organization.

Sixteenth and seventeenth century Europe was also pushing out the frontiers of settlement; its geographical boundaries were bursting. This was an era of colonization to many areas—among them, America. Settlers came to these new lands from Spain, from France, from Britain, and (earlier) from Portugal. The Spanish and the Portuguese settled in South and Central America—the Portuguese on the east, in what is now Brazil, the Spanish on the west, up through Central America, and as far north as Florida. The French came, settling what is today Canada, traveling down around the Great Lakes, and following the Mississippi River to its mouth at what is now New Orleans. The British, who came last, settled the coastal strip of America from Maine almost to the Florida border. The Colonists came over for reasons as varied as their nationalities and their temperaments—for freedom of worship, for escape from political persecution, but also purely and simply for the sake of a business venture. Obviously, the settlers who came

[1] Economies of scale means that as the output of a firm increases, its costs per unit of output fall. The growing size of the market made possible larger firms. The optimum size of the firm changes with technology and has generally grown larger with modern technology.

were adventurous people. The whole undertaking involved risks unthinkable to any but the most daring; and this is reflected in the social attitudes of the Colonists who came. Theirs was the determination to better themselves, to build a new life. The dissidents among them were continually struggling to improve not just the religious and political climates, but the economic climate as well. One of the main prerequisites to development—lacking today in some underdeveloped countries, but one that we richly inherited— is the combination of social attitudes that attuned America's Colonists to economic growth; they responded to incentives that made the markets for labor and capital work better, and they tried to produce goods and services in demand elsewhere.

The products of the Colonial economy were those that they could make most efficiently. What a given area tends to produce efficiently will be determined by the relative costs of the four factors of production: land, labor, capital, and managerial talents. Those must be put together in some form to produce anything. The cost of each of these productive factors is determined by its scarcity or abundance and its availability. Abundance tends to lower the price; scarcity elevates it, as potential users bid higher. For example, if not much capital is available, but many people need capital to construct buildings, factories, equipment, and farms, then the price of capital will be high. Similarly, if a great deal of rich, productive land is available, the price of land will be low. This is the pattern that determined the form of production in the New World. Having abundant rich land, scarce labor, and scarce capital, the Colonies not surprisingly turned to agriculture as the major source of economic activity for about 90 per cent of their population. Now set this concept alongside the particular physiographic characteristics of the New World, and it becomes evident why each region developed its own specific economic pattern. Each region's production possibilities were different. The great incentive was to better their living standards by producing goods so efficiently that they would find a market outside the Colonies and so would make possible the import of other goods that they wanted. This desire for efficient production divided the Colonies into three major economic areas: the South, the Middle Colonies, and New England.

The South produced goods, rice, and indigo in the lower part and tobacco in the upper part, which fitted ideally the sort of pattern that England had in mind for colonial settlement; that is, it produced commodities that the English did not produce and that England and other countries wanted. One disadvantage appeared in this pattern, however: these agricultural goods all required not only an abundance of land, but an abundance of labor—and this was a scarce and expensive factor. Indeed, it appears that wages may have been as high in the Colonial area as they were in England, or even higher. This led to the desire to import workers for all the Colonies, but most pressingly for the southern plantations. Early plantation labor was made up of freemen or indentured servants, who gradually were replaced by slaves in the seventeenth century. Southern Colonists accepted slavery as a means of supplying a cheap labor force during that particular period to work on the plantations and to produce major commodities in international demand. The pattern of trade and commerce of the southern Colonies increasingly emphasized the exports of these items, particularly to England and Europe, to finance the import of other goods. In general, the value of their exports exceeded the value of their imports and thus fitted ideally the pattern that Britain hoped to develop with colonial activities.

Turning to the Middle Colonies, we see a very different picture. These comprised the relatively fertile agricultural areas of New York, Pennsylvania, and New Jersey, where grain and livestock could be efficiently produced and where important seaports opened up access to the interior. This was a valuable combination; for at the time, the only efficient way to carry goods was by water. Rich land that lay far from navigable water was handicapped by the high costs of land transport, and it could not offer its products for sale outside its particular area. So New York and Philadelphia grew up as collection centers for the agricultural goods of the interior, as ports for shipping these goods to the rest of the world and importing other goods and services that the Colonists so much wanted. Since the products of the Middle Colonies were by and large the things that the Englishman himself produced, the pattern of trade of these colonies came to be more with southern Europe and the West Indies than directly with England. As a matter of fact, more was imported than exported in the Middle Colonies' trade with England.

The third area, New England, was totally different again.

Although most of the population still earned their living from the soil, the land was relatively poor (except in a few rich river valleys like the Connecticut), and an increasing percentage turned to gaining a living from the sea, which first provided rich fishing resources and whaling. As New Englanders became expert in these skills, their colonies achieved maturity as a major shipping power in the world and as shipbuilders, not only for their own needs, but for England itself. The Colonies were also shipping not only their own goods (like fish) to the West Indies but were picking up and transporting goods all over the British Empire and beyond it, so that shipping income had become a most important factor in the New Englander's well-being.

Over-all, it is clear that the Colonies were genuinely thriving. Probably, on a per capita basis, they were as prosperous as the English people themselves and possibly more so. The sources of their prosperity, by and large, were a thriving agriculture and a resultant vigorous export trade that grew in value and in per capita terms, and an increasing shipping income from carrying other people's goods as well as their own. One problem appeared: the Colonists, intent on raising their living standard, wanted to buy more of the goods of England and the Continent than they could finance by their exports alone, and this resulted in a drain of specie from the Colonies. Paid in gold and silver for goods sold overseas, the luxury-hungry Colonists tended to ship out the specie as soon as it was received, in return for imports. Since these metals were the base of the money supply, the Colonists sometimes complained about being short of money. What they meant was that they preferred to import more goods rather than to keep a better money supply at home.

A deliberate British policy of control of its colonial economy began in the 1650's with the imposition of navigation laws, designed to protect British shipping from the far more efficient shipping of the Dutch. As already noted, the Dutch flute and Dutch shipping were the most efficient then known, increasingly carrying the world's goods. Shipping was too important a source of world income for the British to let it go lightly, and part of their answer to the challenge was the promulgation of laws requiring that ships in

CHART 10. VALUE OF AMERICAN COLONIES' EXPORTS TO ENGLAND, 1697-1776
(In 100,000 pounds sterling)

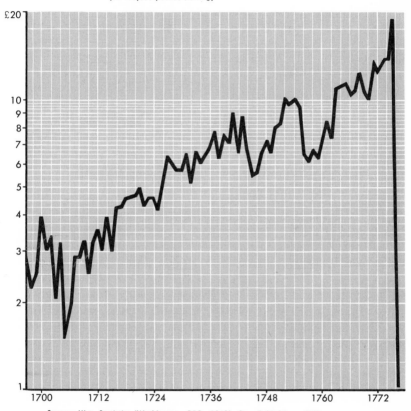

Source: *Hist. Statistics* (Washington: GPO, 1960), Ser. Z 21-34, p. 757.

the British empire trade be built and largely manned by Britons or by British colonials. They required further that certain strategic, or "enumerated," goods be shipped only to England. Tobacco was one of these, and Chart 11 indicates that England benefited handsomely by the receipt of all American tobacco and the re-export of a substantial part of it. It is perhaps not surprising that the Colonists complained about enumeration, which will be discussed more fully later on. Next, the laws demanded that European goods en route to the Colonies had to pass through England and the English customs—another grievance for the import-loving Colonials. Fourth, the Colonies were prohibited from selling manufactures abroad or from exporting many manufactures; this was true of hats and some other products. Fifth, to assure Britain's independent supply of certain important commodities, a bounty was declared on such Colonial products as indigo dye and the naval stores used in all

CHART 11. TOBACCO EXPORTED TO ENGLAND BY AMERICAN
COLONIES, 1697-1775
(In millions of pounds)

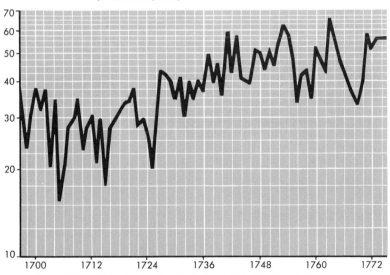

Source: *Hist. Statistics* (Washington: GPO, 1960), Ser. Z 223-29, p. 765.

kinds of naval and merchant marine activities. After 1763, when the British had just struggled through a costly war and their exchequer was depleted, they felt that the Colonists should pay some additional burden. The result was a number of revenue acts with names that are schoolboy history—the Stamp Act, the Townsend Act, the Sugar Act—all designed to increase taxes on the Colonists. Also, measures were passed that were designed primarily to keep the Colonists from crossing the Appalachian Mountains and settling in an area that the British hoped to keep out-of-bounds, to prevent warfare with Indian tribes. This also stirred Colonial antagonism, although no one of these acts was vitally important in terms of its economic impact on the Colonists.

BRITISH POLICY AND COLONIAL WELFARE, 1763-1775

What was the actual economic impact of the total restrictive policy? [2] Presumably, what the British had in mind by the navigation system, the totality of acts that they pursued, was to alter the pattern of world trade and commerce to gain more income for Britain at the expense of other countries. This result was achieved, and Britain captured a good deal of sea transport and trade at the expense primarily of the Dutch, but to some extent, of the French, Spanish, and Portuguese as well. For our purpose, the crux of the question is this: did Britain also gain at the expense of her own Colonies, or in fact did the Colonies themselves participate in the total benefits resulting from this set of policies?

There is no point in being much concerned with the problem before 1763; before that date, it is doubtful that the Colonists could have stood alone or would have wanted to be free. The French always were up north above them, ready to take them over. But after 1763, we can look at a world in which the Colonists might have been either outside or inside the British system. The actual

[2] I would like to acknowledge my indebtedness to my colleague, Robert P. Thomas, as a result of numerous lengthy discussions of the issues involved in this section. See his "A Quantitative Approach to the Study of the Effects of British Imperial Policy upon Colonial Welfare: Some Preliminary Findings," *JEH*, XXV, No. 4 (Dec. 1965).

condition was a world in which they were inside. The hypothetical alternative would be one in which they were an independent nation outside the British system.[3] How would they have fared? Not all the information needed to answer that question is available, so what we find is a partial answer based on what actually occurred in a later period—from 1783, when the Colonies did indeed become independent, until 1793, when all of Europe went to war. This is a roughly comparable period to the one under consideration. Unfortunately, neither an economist nor a historian ever has all the facts he would like in assessing any given period or event. But for this comparison of two periods there is an abundance of clues. What do they add up to in the way of evidence?

First of all, tobacco was a major source of additional income derived by the British from their relationship with us. Indeed, there is no doubt that the passage of tobacco through England resulted in income for the British merchants. Equally, therefore, there is no doubt that tobacco would have returned higher incomes to the Colonial grower had the Colonies been independent, and this is precisely what we see in the period after 1783 when the Confederation period occurs.

But take the next item—shipping. A free and independent nation found out after 1783 that its ability to engage in this lucrative activity was curtailed by the Navigation Acts, not only of Britain, but of all the rest of the countries of Europe. Goods could be shipped between two countries only if they were produced in one of them. But a country like the new American nation, which had become the most efficient shipping nation in the world, lost a great comparative advantage this way. It is therefore probable that America's shipping income would have been lower in the hypothetical case of earlier independence, since the nation would have been excluded from the West Indies trade and also limited in trade with many other parts of the world. Shipbuilding would also have been curtailed, since Britain was a major customer. Other sources of income, our exports of rice and indigo from the lower South,

[3] This is the hypothetical alternative which is usually implicit in a historian's analysis of the issues. In terms of immediate sources of Colonial grievances, however, it was the difference between British policy and enforcement before 1763 and after 1763 that triggered Colonial discontent; the Colonists, at least in the beginning, had in mind as the alternative a return to the conditions that existed prior to 1763.

decreased as a result of independence in the Confederation period.

What about restrictions placed on Colonial manufacturing? They were actually not important. It will be remembered from the earlier discussion of factor proportions that manufacturing requires comparatively large amounts of capital and labor, but little or no land; this happened to be exactly the wrong combination of factors for the Colonial economy which, therefore, could not compete effectively in manufacturing (except where nearness to raw materials gave them a special advantage such as in iron production and shipbuilding). Presumably, little if any income was lost as a result of the British domination.

The final item to consider is the requirement that Colonial imports had to pass through England. Here, the likelihood is that the Colonists would have enjoyed somewhat better terms if they had been independent (and indeed this shows up in the Confederation period as a lowering of import prices from those of the earlier period).

A further examination of the issues involved in assessing the impact of British policy on Colonial welfare will focus upon the unresolved aspects of the problem and perhaps can reduce the degree of uncertainty that we may have about them. No one can study Colonial economic history without being indebted to Lawrence Harper, whose pioneering efforts in gathering Colonial statistics form the basis for much of our resource material today. Moreover, Harper's examination of the incidence of British policy is the most careful that has yet been made, and his essay entitled "The Effect of the Navigation Acts on the Thirteen Colonies"[4] is the classic work upon the subject. Harper approaches the problem by employing the method suggested above; that is, he develops a hypothetical alternative of what might have been had there been no Navigation Acts. He uses the period after America became independent as a yardstick of comparison. While Harper does not have absolute figures on what the income of the Colonies was between 1763 and 1775, and therefore is not comparing actual absolute income with what absolute income would have been under the hypothetical alternative, his method—in view of the lack of data—is equally good. He measures the relative burden and benefits of

[4] In *The Era of the American Revolution,* ed. Richard B. Morris (New York: Columbia Univ., 1939).

the Navigation Acts, and the net result constitutes the difference between what income was and what income would have been. Harper finds that the main costs to the Thirteen Colonies were on tobacco, rice, and importation of European goods, and that the main credits to the Thirteen Colonies from the navigation system were bounties paid on indigo, naval stores, and lumber. His estimates suggest that the net burden upon the Colonies was between $2.5 million and $7 million, depending on which of his estimates one employs. In short, he is suggesting that the income of the Colonists would have been that much higher had there been no Navigation Acts. His table of estimates of the burden and benefits is reproduced as Table 5.[5]

TABLE 5. HARPER'S ESTIMATES OF BURDENS AND BENEFITS

Cost to the Thirteen Colonies		Lowest estimate	Intermediate estimate	Highest estimate
On tobacco		$2,177,000	$2,428,000	$3,401,000
On rice		186,000	231,000	517,000
On European goods		521,000	997,000	3,444,000
		$2,884,000	$3,656,000	$7,362,000
Credit to bounties paid on Colonial products				
On indigo	£23,086			
On naval stores	35,203			
On lumber	6,557			
	£64,846 or			
		—324,000	—324,000	—324,000
		$2,560,000	$3,332,000	$7,038,000

Source: Harper, op. cit., p. 37.

[5] Harper correctly allows no weight to manufacturing restrictions on the Colonists, which clearly were no significant burden. Likewise, the taxes collected after 1763 by the Revenue Acts, which caused such discontent among the Colonists, were not an appreciable amount.

Harper's work is certainly the starting point for any serious student to re-evaluate the set of issues involved, but his results are basically deficient on three scores and therefore require very substantial revisions: (1) he did not precisely delineate the hypothetical alternative that would have existed; (2) his implicit economic analysis is deficient in some crucial respects; and (3) the statistical data that he employed and that were available to him at that time are in need of very sharp revision at several points. We shall examine each in turn.

The correct hypothetical alternative for the American Colonies between 1763 and 1775 is that of being outside the British imperial system, compared to being a part of it. Harper's direct measures of burdens and benefits include only a part of this total difference.[6] Perhaps the most critical omission is that the Colonists received substantial income from carrying goods to and from the British West Indies, and therefore shipping income would have been reduced by being outside the system.[7] Ship sales to Britain were another loss. The most important shortcoming in Harper's hypothetical alternative is that of protection. He mentions in his concluding paragraph that the Colonists received many other advantages, including military and naval protection, but he assigns no weight to them. Yet, as a matter of fact, an independent America would have had to pay for military and naval protection of its own; and when it gained independence it was forced to expend over $2

[6] Harper's problem is that he does not use a single consistent hypothetical alternative. The correct alternative must be what the Colonists fought a war to achieve—a nation independent of the British—which meant freedom not only from the burdens of British policy but also from the benefits of sheltered and protected markets and trade in a mercantilistic world of restrictions against free trade.

[7] Total exports to the West Indies (British and foreign) do not appear to have dropped, since the fall in exports to the British West Indies was countered by a rise to the West Indian possessions of the other European powers. To determine the actual loss in the West Indies trade would necessitate information on the amount of smuggling in the West Indies. Also, to the extent that the men and capital formerly employed in shipping were employed in other economic pursuits, the net loss is the difference in productivity between their employment in shipping and in other activities.

million a year for armed forces facing the Indians on the frontier and for naval protection for its shipping.[8]

The second shortcoming is in the implicit economic analysis. Harper assumes a perfectly inelastic demand for the commodities: that is, he is assuming that the same amount of the commodities would have been sold at prices different from those that existed. This is very unlikely; and the more responsive the quantity would have been to changes in price, the greater the difference would have been between the actual results and those that he specifies. Thus if the price in Amsterdam were now 2 cents per pound lower, we want to know how much more tobacco the Dutch would have bought.[9] The second deficiency in his economic analysis is that he assumes that the bounty paid to the Colonists was a net gain, and in fact that is not so. To take the illustration of the bounty paid upon indigo: he assumes that £23,000 a year paid on indigo was a net credit to the Colonies. In fact, the net amount is really the difference between the amount that the British paid and what that land, labor, and capital devoted to indigo production would have earned in the next best alternative pursued. It is this difference that is the net gain to the Colonists. Needless to say, this is a much smaller figure.

Finally, his economic analysis is deficient in that he uses the period all the way up until the 1840's to compare to the periods before the American Revolution. Actually, the conditions of supply and demand in the American economy changed so radically after 1793, with the advent of the French and Napoleonic wars, that comparisons after that date are really meaningless. The proper period for comparison should be between 1783 and 1793, and more properly from about 1785 to 1793, since one should allow several years after the Revolutionary War as a period of economic readjustment.

[8] The government spent annually $2,132,898 for national defense in the first nine years after ratification of the Constitution. This does not include the additional costs of conducting an independent foreign policy (foreign ministers, etc.). Our celebrated struggles with the Barbary pirates are only one case in point.

[9] This is true both of the amount demanded and of the amount that would have been supplied. That is, if the price the planter received had been higher, how much more would he have produced?

The third major deficiency in Harper's study is in the statistical data. Harper suggests that shipping earnings would have been higher under the alternative and cites the percentage of goods carried in American bottoms in 1790 as 80 per cent of the total of goods carried. This figure is in error; actually, it was little more than 50 per cent of the total. A far more serious problem is in the prices that Harper uses in measuring the burden on tobacco, rice, and imports. He estimates the burden on the Colonies by looking at the difference between the price that existed before the Revolution and the price that existed after the Revolution. He adjusts the figure by changes in the general price levels; however, subsequent research since the publication of his essay [10] results in very different and much smaller differential price figures. Harper estimates that the Colonists would have enjoyed a tobacco price of 2½ to 3¼ cents per pound higher had they been able to trade directly with the Dutch, but more recent figures suggest that the price differential would have been between ½ and 1½ cents per pound. The result would have been to lower the burden upon American tobacco. The same would hold for the case of rice and on imported goods.

The tentative conclusions one would draw from this re-examination would be to dramatically reduce the burden of British policy on the American Colonies in the pre-Revolutionary period; and indeed this very tentative conclusion is consistent with recent research on the Confederation period, which suggests that the export income, perhaps the main independent determinant of changing income of that period, was probably no higher in the late 1780's than it had been in the period 1770 to 1775, suggesting that the newly independent nation was at best about as well off as the Colonists had been in that critical era.[11]

[10] N.W. Posthumus, *Inquiry into the History of Prices in Holland* (Leiden: E.J. Brill, 1946).

[11] Gordon C. Bjork, "The Weaning of the American Economy: Independence, Market Changes, and Economic Development," *JEH*, XXIV, No. 4 (Dec. 1964), 541-60; and Albert Fishlow, "Discussion," *JEH*, XXIV, No. 4 (Dec. 1964), 561-66.

chapter 4

THE
YEARS OF DECISION,
1783-1793

The years 1783 to 1793 were a time of decision for the new American society. Politically, this was the period for choosing the form of a new government and for establishing a Constitution, which has lasted ever since. It is equally true that for the economy these were years of decision, for developing the basic "rules of the game" that have continued right to this day.

The year 1776 produced not one but two documents of importance to the new nation. Both have had fundamental significance for our history. One was, of course, the Declaration of Independence, pointing the way to political freedom; the other was the publication in England of Adam Smith's *The Wealth of Nations.* Here was a concept of an economic order, analyzing the way a market economy works and indicating an unshackled system of enterprise as the logical way to achieve "the wealth of nations."

When the war with England ceased, America faced all the problems that confront any new nation. To survive, it was necessary to create a viable economy. A government must be established not only for the political process and voting rights but to be concerned with countless other decisions, not the least of them of economic origin. What should be the government's role in the economy? What responsibility should it have? How should a legal structure be developed to delineate the rights and the restrictions of private property? Where were tax monies to come from, and how much? Also to be decided were the touchy issues of where the money should be spent. To speak of taxes is to pose a double question: who is to pay them and who is to benefit from them? When tax receipts are paid out, some people will usually be more advantaged than others. Finally, a monetary system was needed not only to serve as the fiscal agent for the government but also to provide a medium of exchange and to develop efficient capital markets necessary to a market economy.

Historically, these questions had been answered by setting up the system—or at least the organized procedure—known as mercantilism, in which the government was involved in the economy in a whole variety of ways. Among other mercantilistic devices, bounties were paid to encourage the production of specified commodities, and monopolistic privileges were awarded to some companies, giving exclusive trading rights in particular areas. The aim was for the government and the economy jointly to promote the national expansion and welfare—and this, as noted earlier, at the expense of other countries.

Now came Adam Smith's diametrically opposite view attacking mercantilism, arguing that it was an inefficient system, one that fostered monopoly, one that encouraged inefficiency, one that gave special privileges to particular groups in the society. He found it to be the very antithesis of how a society should be organized to give maximum wealth for the people of that nation. Smith argued that the main basis for economic growth was specialization and division of labor. Efficiency stemmed from the employment of enough people to produce a given commodity, so that their tasks could be specialized, each person having a particular function. The more specialized the task, the more rapidly and efficiently it could be done, and the more a man could concentrate on doing just that one thing repetitively. Also, if his specialized task were reduced to its narrowest possible form, an act performed with his hands, then machines could be developed to do his work. In short, technological change would be encouraged by specialization; and since division of labor depends on the feasibility of producing on a large enough scale, we come to the size of the market as a basic influence upon specialization and division of labor. A small producer, turning out just a few items a day, a week, or a year, will probably do all the work himself; but if his market enlarges, he will need to have a large number of workers. Each task can be specialized, and he can then institute division of labor.

In a market economy, the one who organizes the economic activity is the entrepreneur or businessman. It is he who decides what will be produced, basing his decision on the relative profitability of different kinds of pursuits. If it appears that making shoes will be more profitable than making bricks, or hats, or any other alternatives, he will produce shoes; but to start making shoes, he needs a location, equipment, and labor. Accordingly, he borrows the necessary capital to buy machines, to build a factory, and to advance payment to his workers while they are producing the goods. While the entrepreneur makes the decisions about what will be produced (being guided by relative profitability), the capital market plays a crucial role in financing his start in production.

Adam Smith was a bitter critic of mercantilism because he saw in it an artificial inducement for a society to produce the wrong things. Because bounties or subsidies were paid for a certain commodity, it might appear to an entrepreneur as a profitable venture, when in reality it was a very inefficient production. The relative profitability of different kinds of activity not only is an advantageous guide to the businessman, but also it is consistent with expanding the welfare of the society as a whole—that is, the most profitable pursuits are those in which efficiency and output can be most increased in response to what consumers want, and therefore they are most beneficial to the society.[1] It was this that led Adam Smith to the conclusion that private self-interest—guiding the businessman into the most profitable pursuits, the worker to the job with the highest wages, and so forth—will, by the same process, promote maximum public welfare.

This conflict between Adam Smith's view and the world of mercantilism was very much in the minds of Americans in the 1780's as they struggled to resolve the many problems they faced.

---

[1] Adam Smith was aware of important exceptions to the equation of private rates of return with social ones. This issue and its significance for the role of government are discussed in Chapter 8.

Some of these problems were of staggering size. The new nation had emerged from the Revolutionary War deeply in debt, not only to foreigners such as the French who had helped fight the war with finances, munitions, and equipment, but also in domestic debt to citizens who had loaned the Continental Congress great sums. These debts were of such magnitude that the question was how could we pay them all. And, indeed, should they all be paid? The latter was considered a reasonable question because, in many cases, the original creditors had sold their Continental bonds at a fraction of their face value; and it was argued that since speculators had bought up these bonds at a substantial discount, they should not receive payment at face value. The whole knotty problem of the public debt was the subject of priority debate in America's early government.

A second problem facing the economy was that the soldiers of the Revolutionary War had been promised substantial benefits. In previous wars, it had been a policy to award officers half pay for life after a war, or to pay them full pay for five years after the war. Again, who would pay for this? And where were the taxes to come from that would be needed for such payment?

Still a third urgent need of tax monies after the war arose from the fact that our shipping and trade now became the prey of pirates—particularly the Barbary pirates when we tried to enter the Mediterranean. Before the war, the Colonies had been sheltered under the British agreement that, in effect, paid tribute to these buccaneers to safeguard British and Colonial ships. Now free and a good prey to the pirates, we faced two alternatives: to pay similar tribute or to build a navy and attempt to defeat the Barbary pirates. Either choice involved a substantial amount of money.

An even more basic point remained to be decided. Should the American economy be steered toward mercantilism? Should bounties and subsidies be paid to encourage certain industries? Should manufacturing be expanded even though unprofitable to avoid dependence on foreign countries, or should a free market decide? The conflict between Adam Smith and the mercantilist philosophy had reached these shores.

All of these were vital issues of the 1780's, and the attempt to resolve them was part and parcel of the process of thinking out the needs of the new government that anticipated the American Constitution and the Constitutional Convention of 1787. An event occurred that encouraged a more rapid resolution of these problems than might otherwise have taken place. In 1787, a former captain in the Revolutionary War, Daniel Shays, led a group of discontented Massachusetts farmers in revolt against the burdens of taxation that they felt were lying unduly heavily on the farmers of western Massachusetts and from which they felt they received very few benefits. Shays' Rebellion shook the new American society, shocking the people into realization of how fragile was the structure of law and order, and how necessary it was for the problems to be resolved—the same problems of taxation previously blamed on the British. Shays' Rebellion also pointed up the need for a unified policy among all the states. Heretofore, in the period of the Confederation, each state had made independent decisions, particularly with respect to port entry fees for foreign ships, tonnage duties, and a variety of other commercial activities. This had, of course, led to competitive lowering of rates among the states.

The idea of a stronger central government gradually emerged as the answer to these needs, and this led to calling a convention initially aimed at overhauling the Articles of Confederation, but which ultimately focused on creating a whole new framework and a new set of conditions.

Of all the bookshelves of volumes written about the Constitutional Convention, one that has profoundly shaped our concept of the period is that of Charles Beard, *The Economic Interpretation of the Constitution*. Looking at the background of the people who dominated the Convention, Beard contended that they wrote a Constitution aimed at protecting their own interests. Motives are a difficult thing to assess in history, and I have no intention of entering this controversy, because, for one thing, I am not sure that it is a very useful one. It is hard to say with any confidence whether a man makes a policy because of narrow immediate interests or because his fundamental view about how the society's economy ought to be organized happens to lead him to that set of policies.

What we really want to look at with respect to the Constitution is the sum of its results, viewing it by somewhat the same standards that Adam Smith uses in examining how an economy ought to work. Smith never believed that individual decisions of businessmen and workers were motivated by anything but their own selfish desires for better standards of living. He even believed such men would have promoted monopoly if they could. But what he did conclude was that the net result of the interaction of all these individual self-interests turned out to be a society that produced the greatest improvements in welfare and the greatest growth that one could get.

The Constitution itself, however narrowly or broadly it was related to the self-interests of our forefathers, turned out to be a very effective instrument both for political democracy and economic development. In the economic field, some notable achievements of the Constitution were these. First and foremost, by delegating to the central government the power to levy taxes, it made possible the undertaking of necessary continuing functions of federal authority. Among other things, the government could now redeem the debts incurred during the Revolutionary War; and assuming the debts of the states, it was in a position to pay them off. This was a significant step in establishing a capital market, since it gave investors confidence that loans would be repaid. Second, the Constitution assigned to the federal government the right to coin money and the pre-eminent power over the money supply. In this area, many court decisions were required to clarify the meaning of the Constitution; but the long-run result was to provide a uniform, centrally controlled monetary system—something viewed from our perspective as essential. The federal government was also given authority over foreign affairs, so that tariffs and negotiations of treaties and agreements were no longer within the power of the individual states. Interstate commerce was another area delegated to the government, and this control over goods moving from one state to another has historically, and to this day, had enormous impact on the role of the federal government in economic activities. By prohibiting states from erecting barriers to the interstate movement of goods, this clause not only encouraged the growth of a national market, but it has also been a major wedge giving the federal government constitutional authority to exercise control and regulation over economic activity.

It should be emphasized, however, that the most important contribution of the Constitution was not in specific decisions made (though these are important), but rather that it set the ground rules for future decisions. It defined the protection of private property and the enforcement of contracts; it created a system of stability, of law and order, which reduced uncertainty—and returning to Adam Smith's views, it is obvious how important stability is for the functioning of this market economy. What makes the businessman willing to invest is the expectation of profits, discounted for risks. If there is a high risk potential, then profits must be still higher in order to induce the businessman to invest, and the higher the uncertainty or risk, the fewer willing investors. Accordingly, as established by the Constitution, this climate of maintaining stability, of reducing uncertainty, of recognizing the rights of property and the enforcement of contracts was most vital and conducive to making a market economy work well.

In 1789, when the new government came into existence it immediately set about to rectify some of the pressing problems remaining from the Confederation period. It established uniform tonnage duties of 50 cents a ton on foreign vessels and of 6 cents a ton on U.S. vessels. The differential was a way of encouraging our shipping, and giving us a bargaining weapon in negotiating with foreign countries to reduce or to repeal their widespread discriminatory legislation against this country. A tariff was also passed as a source of revenue; and indeed the early tariff became the main source of revenue of the new nation, providing funds to operate the government. The tariff was only incidentally protective, although there were some who desired protection. At this time, too, Alexander Hamilton, who was really the architect of so much of the early economic policy in the new nation, wrote a series of famous reports which influenced our subsequent economic policies. His "Report on Manufactures" became a classic; in it, he recommended the encouragement of manufacturing under a system of bounties and subsidies. Although this report had no immediate effect (and indeed harked back to mercantilist views), it did contain valuable insights into our economy, and it turned out to point the way of American industrial development. Hamilton's "Report on Public Credit" laid the groundwork for the assumption of state debts and for issuing bonds that would then pay off the debtors; these bonds, in turn, being circulated as a medium of credit to underlie issuance of other bonds, and of loans, so that the whole process formed a credit base for a society. This device was important to creating a better capital market, something we have already observed as essential in improving economic organization. Hamilton was also instrumental in paving the way toward creation of the First United States Bank, which became the means of tying the banks of the country to an over-all monetary system. Opening with an initial subscription of $10 million, of which the government contributed $2 million, this became, in a sense, a bankers' bank. It acted as an agent of the government, assisting in spreading and strengthening the entire banking system, thus helping immeasurably in improving the capital market.

It would be a mistake to think of Alexander Hamilton as a disciple of Adam Smith. He was too much of a mercantilist to fit that mold, and the policies he recommended (particularly in the "Report on Manufactures") involved a degree of government intervention that was the very subject of *The Wealth of Nations'* attack. But the policies of Hamilton that *were adopted* were those that provided the essential economic structure to make a market economy work more effectively. Their result was to reduce uncertainty and to help create the essential conditions for an efficient capital market.

THE ECONOMY, 1783-1793, PROSPERITY OR DEPRESSION

In the turbulent decade of the 1780's, contemporaries argued vigorously about the state of the economy. Some pictured the economy in dismal and serious depression; others maintained that its present and future prospects were not nearly so bad—indeed, that they looked rather bright. Hamilton was a leading exponent of the sad state into which the economy had fallen, and I quote at some length from *The Federalist*, Paper 15, where he describes the plight of the economy before the new Constitution.

> We may indeed with propriety be said to have reached almost the last stage of national humiliation. There is scarcely anything that can wound the pride or degrade the character of an independent nation which we do not experience. Are there engage-

ments to the performance of which we are held by every tie respectable among men? These are the subjects of constant and unblushing violation. Do we owe debts to foreigners and to our own citizens contracted in a time of imminent peril for the preservation of our political existence? These remain without any proper or satisfactory provision for their discharge. . . . Are we in a condition to resent or to repel the aggression? We have neither troops, nor treasury, nor government. Are we even in a condition to remonstrate with dignity? . . . Are we entitled by nature and compact to a free participation in the navigation of the Mississippi? Spain excludes us from it. Is public credit an indispensable resource in time of public danger? We seem to have abandoned its cause as desperate and irretrievable. Is commerce of importance to national wealth? Ours is at the lowest point of declension. Is respectability in the eyes of foreign powers a safeguard against foreign encroachments? The imbecility of our government even forbids them to treat with us. Our ambassadors abroad are the mere pageants of mimic sovereignty. . . . To shorten an enumeration of particulars which can afford neither pleasure nor instruction, it may in general be demanded, what indication is there of national disorder, poverty, and insignificance that could befall a community so peculiarly blessed with natural advantages as we are, which does not form a part of the dark catalogue of our public misfortunes.[2]

On the other hand, Benjamin Franklin, returning to America after a long absence in 1785, felt that the position of the economy was not nearly as dismal as had been described to him. But since most polemical statements are made in the context of some specific policy orientation, such statements are no substitute for careful analytical examination of the conditions of the Confederation in the 1780's. The argument among historians has continued right up to the present date. Currently, one of the leading authorities on the period, Merrill Jensen, maintains that the period of Confederation was a period of vigorous growth for the newly independent nation, freed from the shackles of British imperial policy.[3] On the other

[2] Alexander Hamilton, John Jay, James Madison, *The Federalist: A Commentary on the Constitution of the United States* (New York: Modern Library, 1937), pp. 87-88.

[3] *The New Nation* (New York: Knopf, 1950). Jensen quotes approvingly an earlier study that "by 1790 the United States had far outstripped the colonies of a few short years before" (p. 218) and goes on to conclude: "By

hand, Curtis Nettels views the period as one dominated by depression and slow recovery of the economy.[4] So far, the argument has been fought on the basis of odd statistics here and there and quotations such as those of Franklin and Hamilton cited above; and at this level, arguments continue *ad infinitum.* The only solution is to develop the necessary statistical data to tell us what did happen in these critical years. Ideally, we need national income and per capita income figures in order to be able to say precisely what occurred. Such figures are not available, but a beginning in the direction of more precisely delineating the economic contours of the period has been made by Gordon Bjork [5] in developing estimates of exports and imports, and of the prices of exports and imports, over the years 1783 to 1790. When these are taken in conjunction with the balance-of-payments figures that exist from 1790 on, we can get some idea of the period. We are assuming that the portion of the American people who were not in the market—those who were living on the frontier or were simply not producing for the market —experienced no change in welfare and real income over the decade. Then we must further examine what happened to the market sector, and the leading determinant of income there would be the export sector of the economy.[6] Bjork has re-estimated the

---

1790 the export of agricultural produce was double what it had been before the war. American cities grew rapidly, with the result that housing was scarce and building booms produced a labor shortage. Tens of thousands of farmers spread outwards to the frontiers. There can be no question but that freedom from the British Empire resulted in a surge of activity in all phases of American life (p. 424).

[4] Curtis P. Nettels, *The Emergence of a National Economy, 1775-1815* (New York: Holt, 1962), chaps. iii, iv.

[5] Bjork, *JEH*, XXIV, 541-60.

[6] It is important to make explicit the model that underlies this statement, in the hope that subsequent research can test the model and its underlying assumptions. The assumptions are that: (1) there was no change in per capita well-being of those in the nonmarket sector; (2) changes in income from the export sector were the major independent influence upon income in the market sector in the years 1783-1793; and (3) to the extent that a fall in output in the export sector led to a shifting of labor and capital into the local market or into the nonmarket sectors, to that extent labor and capital were less efficiently employed than in the export sector.

Since population in the three largest cities increased by only 3 per cent, while total population increased by 40 per cent, between 1775 and 1790, the evidence is consistent with proposition 2 and with the fact that, of necessity, there was some shift back to the nonmarket sector.

value of British trade with the United States in terms of market value of British imports from the U.S. between 1770 and 1792.[7] It is evident (Table 6) that trade with Britain in the 1780's was not as great as it had been before the Revolution. Was this loss made up in trade with other countries? Total value of exports in 1770 was £3,165,000.[8] Bjork has gone on to make crude estimates of the total value of exports based on partial data from the States between 1784 and 1792 (Table 7).

The other major item acting as a credit to the balance of payments was shipping earnings, and here we must do more guess work. We have no existing published estimates of shipping earnings either

TABLE 6. BRITISH IMPORTS FROM THE UNITED STATES, 1770-1792

Year	Estimated market value (in thousands)
1770	$3,248
1771	5,978
1772	5,078
1773	4,960
1774	4,842
1775	6,555
1784	4,429
1785	4,901
1786	4,134
1787	4,488
1788	4,901
1789	4,901
1790	4,905
1791	4,724
1792	4,311

Source: Bjork, JEH, XXIV, 550.

in 1770 or in the 1780's, although we do have estimates of shipping earnings from 1790 on. A major study underway, using data on freight rates gathered in a study of ocean shipping suggests, how-

[7] Bjork, *JEH*, XXIV, 550.
[8] James Shepherd, "A Balance of Payments for the Thirteen Colonies, 1768-1772: A Summary," *JEH*, XXV, No. 4 (Dec. 1965).

ever, that with the available data, estimates of shipping earnings in 1770 range somewhere between \$2.5 million and \$5 million.[9]

We have no estimates of shipping earnings for the 1780's, and as yet no work has been done on the subject, but all of the contemporary qualitative descriptions suggest that shipping was badly hurt during the Confederation period. This view is borne out by evidence of the fall-off in shipping to the West Indies and of the dire effect of navigation acts of various countries. Moreover, it is clear that shipbuilding in New England fell off dramatically in the early and middle 1780's, mirroring the difficult state of the shipping industry. It is also clear that, in the last part of the 1780's, shipping earnings were once more expanding, until by 1790, when we again have figures, they had reached almost \$6 million. Thus it is clear that in the 1780's they were substantially smaller. A very liberal estimate would put them in 1785 at around \$4 million. We should note, however, that population is growing throughout this period; and if a figure is expected to give some crude idea of per capita well-being, it must reflect the *per capita* credit for the balance of payments. If we assume that shipping earnings were \$4 million in 1770, then per capita credits of the balance of payments were more than \$9.00. In 1785, if we assume shipping earnings of \$4 million and take Bjork's rough approximation of export credits, our per capita credits were a little more than \$6.50, and by 1790 the figure went up to a little more than \$7.00.[10]

[9] This estimate is arrived at by taking the total outward-bound tonnage of the Colonies in 1770, which was 351,000 tons, and estimating the proportion of this owned by the Colonies to be 33 per cent of that going to Great Britain and Ireland, 50 per cent of that going to southern Europe and Africa, 100 per cent of that going to the West Indies, and 20 per cent of that going to the Americas, Bermuda, and the Bahamas, and then estimating annual earnings of between £3 and £5 per ton, based on freight-rate data from a forthcoming study of the costs of ocean transportation, 1600-1914. Moreover, since ships making trips to the West Indies averaged at least two voyages per year, the tonnage figure for the West Indies was halved. The figure of \$2.5 million is clearly a lower-limit figure, and it is reasonable to assume that shipping earnings were closer to \$5 million, since an average annual earning per ton of £3 is too low. For further discussion, see James Shepherd, "A Balance of Payments for the Thirteen Colonies, 1768-1772" (forthcoming Ph.D. dissertation, U. of Washington).

[10] Douglass C. North, "Early National Income Estimates of the United States," *EDCC*, IX, No. 3 (April 1961), 390.

TABLE 7. ESTIMATED VALUE OF EXPORTS BY STATE, 1784-1792

State	1784	1785	1786	1787	1788
Georgia	$2,148	$1,892	$2,303	$2,717	$2,551
South Carolina			506		
North Carolina					
Virginia					
Maryland					
Delaware					
Pennsylvania	3,725	2,509	2,059	2,142	2,427
New Jersey					
New York					1,925
Connecticut					
Rhode Island					
Massachusetts				1,588	1,969
New Hampshire					
Official total value of exports, in $000					
Ratio estimate of total value of exports in $000,000's	18.9	14.2	14.4	14.4	15.5

Source: Bjork, JEH, XXIV, 548.

These are very crude estimates, and any implications to be drawn from them must be carefully qualified. In order to have any stronger conviction about them, we must know what happened to price levels over this period. We must know whether a given amount of exports bought more or less imports.[11] And finally, we want to known whether the ratio between the export sector and the domestic sectors stayed constant over this period or whether some of our resources shifted into the domestic sector. But allowing for all of these qualifications and misgivings, the very tentative conclusion to be drawn *at this stage of our knowledge* and until data have been further developed is to suggest that the period of Confederation was one in which at least the export-sector income

[11] Bjork estimates that in the 1780's the terms of trade "were very favorable to the United States" and therefore a given amount of exports bought more imports than they had previously. Bjork, *JEH*, XXIV.

1789-90	1790-91	1791-92	Average proportion of trade by states (Per cent) 1790-92
$	$ 491	$ 459	2.4
	2,693	2,428	12.9
	525	528	2.6
	3,132	3,553	16.8
2,028	2,240	2,624	12.2
	120	134	0.6
3,511	3,436	3,821	18.2
	27	23	0.1
2,000	2,505	2,536	12.7
	710	880	4.0
	470	698	2.9
	2,520	2,888	13.6
	143	181	0.8
17,450	19,012	20,753	

17.5

fell from the level reached in the 1770's but was gradually reviving
and improving throughout the 1780's, although even by 1790 it had
not reached the per capita figure achieved in 1770.[12] Such a picture
fits neither the gloomy description by Nettels of a depressed economy nor the buoyant portrayal by Jensen of a growing economy,
doing better now that it was outside the shackles of British policy;[13] rather, it presents a more cautious view of an economy re-
organizing itself, developing its own new export sector and earnings,
and gradually emerging from the problems of readjustment throughout the 1780's and early 1790's.

[12] A better way to treat the problem would be by region, since there was
wide disparity in the movement of the exports of each region.

[13] In one respect, however, the information does support Jensen's position:
the economy was already expanding before the advent of the Constitution, and
the immediate influence of that document was not a major impetus to recovery.

chapter 5

AMERICAN EXPANSION IN A WORLD AT WAR, 1790-1815

By 1790, the political crisis had been resolved, and the economy was enjoying more prosperity than it had known since pre-Revolutionary days. Certainly with unlimited supply of rich lands and an energetic populace, its long-run prospects appeared excellent. Yet there was no immediate prospect of very rapid growth. The reason for this paradox was that the domestic economy was then so small and scattered that the home market was very limited, while the foreign market was circumscribed by the Navigation Acts and by the mercantilist policies of the countries with which the new nation dealt.

The population in 1790 was less than four million, of whom almost 700,000 were slaves. It was almost evenly divided between North and South, with somewhat more than 200,000 living across the mountains in new territories that had just been opened. Only 5 per cent of the people were listed as urban. There were no cities of 50,000, and only two between 25,000 and 50,000—New York and Philadelphia. This small and scattered population did not provide a very substantial market for expansion. Of that great majority of the populace who did not live in cities, most were not a part of the market, since they neither produced crops for sale nor bought commodities on any regular basis.

We have already observed the vicissitudes of the new nation's foreign trade. While it expanded and grew from the lean years of the early 1780's, on a per capita basis it was still well below the prosperous years that preceded the Revolution. Thomas Jefferson in his capacity as Secretary of State summarized some of the obstacles to our trade.

First. In Europe—

Our bread stuff is at most times under prohibitory duties in England, and considerably dutied on re-exportation from Spain to her colonies.

Our tobaccos are heavily dutied in England, Sweden, France and prohibited in Spain and Portugal.

Our rice is heavily dutied in England and Sweden and prohibited in Portugal.

Our fish and salted provisions are prohibited in England, and under prohibitory duties in France.

Our whale oils are prohibited in England and Portugal. And our vessels are denied naturalization in England, and of late, in France.

Second. In the West Indies—

All intercourse is prohibited with the possession of Spain and Portugal.

Our salted provisions and fish are prohibited by England.

Our salted pork and breadstuff (except maize) are received under temporary laws only in the dominions of France, and our salted fish pays there a weighty duty.

Third. In the article of navigation—

Our own carriage of our own tobacco is heavily dutied in Sweden, and lately in France.

We can carry no article, not of our own production, to the British ports in Europe. Nor even our own produce to her American possessions.

. . . Our ships, though purchased and navigated by their own subjects, are not permitted to be used, even in their trade with us.

While the vessels of other nations are secured by standing laws, which cannot be altered but by the concurrent will of the three branches of the British legislature, in carrying thither any produce or manufacture of the country to which they belong, which may be lawfully carried in any vessels, ours, with the same prohibition of what is foreign, are further prohibited by a standing law (12 Car. 2, 18. sect. 3.) from carrying thither all and any of our own domestic productions and manufactures. A subsequent act, indeed, has authorized their executive to permit the carriage of our own productions in our own bottoms at its sole discretion; and the permission has been given from year to year by proclamation, but subject every moment to be withdrawn on that single will, in which event, our vessels, having any thing on board, stand interdicted from the entry of all British ports. The disadvantage of a tenure which may be so suddenly discontinued was experienced by our merchants on a late occasion (April 12, 1792) when an official notification that this law would be strictly enforced, gave them just apprehensions for the fate of their vessels and cargoes despatched or destined to the ports of Great Britain. The minister of that court, indeed, frankly expressed his personal conviction, that the words of the order went farther than was intended, and so he afterwards officially informed us; but the embarrassments of the moment were real and great, and the possibility of their renewal lays our commerce to that country under the same species of discouragement as to other countries, where it is regulated by a single legislator; and the distinction is too remarkable not to be noticed, that our navigation is excluded from the security of fixed laws, while that security is given to the navigation of others.

Our vessels pay in their ports one shilling and nine pence, sterling, per ton, light and trinity dues, more than is paid by British ships, except in the port of London, where they pay the same as British.

The greater part of what they receive from us is re-exported to other countries, under the useless charges of an intermediate deposite, and double voyage.[1]

Even in shipping, where America had an obvious comparative advantage over other countries, only 59 per cent of her trade was carried in American bottoms in 1790, and only 63 per cent by 1792.

The year 1793 was a doubly significant one in American economic history. In that year, Eli Whitney invented the cotton gin, with the resultant expansion of that semi-tropical commodity to dominate the South and to become a main source of economic activity in the United States. More immediately of importance to

[1] Thomas Jefferson, "Report of Secretary of State on the privileges and restrictions on the commerce of the United States in foreign countries." Report to the 3d Cong., 1st Sess., Dec. 16, 1793, printed in *American State Papers, 1789-1794*, I (Boston, 1817), 431-32; 428.

our economy was the outbreak of Britain's war with France, a war
that was to last with one major interruption all the way until 1814.
The conflict tied up shipping and trade of England, France, and
most of the countries in Europe, leaving to the neutral United

CHART 12. VALUE OF EXPORTS AND RE-EXPORTS FROM U.S., 1790-1815

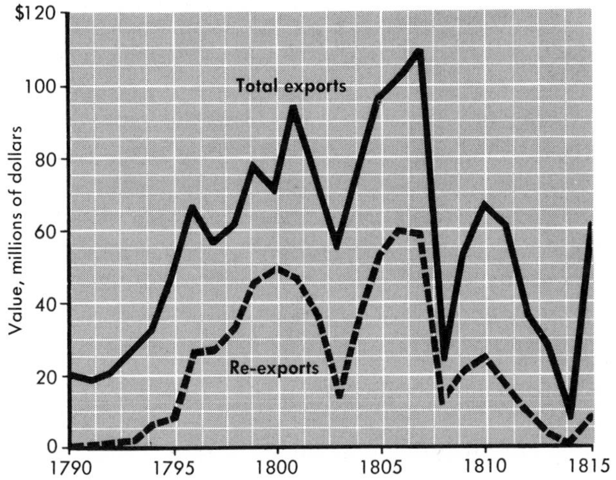

Source: Douglass C. North, *The Economic Growth of the United States, 1790-1860*, p. 26.

States an overwhelming advantage in carrying on most of the
world's trade. At one fell swoop, all the restrictions of Navigation
Acts and mercantilist policies were removed from the American
carrying trade. We transported sugar, coffee, cocoa, pepper, spices,
and other commodities from the tropical and subtropical parts of
the world to Europe, and in turn brought manufactured goods
from Europe to the rest of the world. On top of that, our own
domestic exports increased, particularly as cotton spread over the
South in the wake of the demand from the new cotton textile mills
growing apace in England. The results can be seen in the following
two charts. Chart 12 shows the growth of total exports and re-exports: goods were brought into the United States and then re-
exported to Europe, or brought from Europe and re-exported to

CHART 13.   NET FREIGHT EARNINGS OF U.S. CARRYING TRADE, 1790-1815

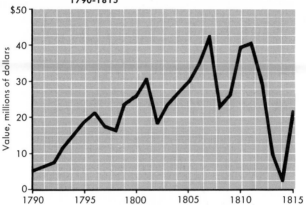

Source: Douglass C. North, *The Economic Growth of the United States, 1790-1860*, p. 28.

colonies. Chart 13 indicates the growth of net shipping earnings from the U.S. carrying trade.

In addition to the rapid expansion in earnings, prices paid for our exports now bought more imports than before, because the price of imports had not risen as much as that of exports. The effect on our terms of trade is seen in Chart 14.[2]

This expansion of trade and shipping was not accomplished without severe trial and tribulations. Both sides in the war were unhappy with America's role; and in 1797 and 1798, French seizures of our ships on the one hand and talks of peace on the other led to a fall in shipping activities. Peace came in 1801, and until 1803 there was another precipitous drop in our activity as European nations again carried their own trade. From 1803 to 1807 the United States experienced another period of turbulent expansion. The end was already in sight in 1805, however, with the Essex decision, in which the British reverted to a 1756 rule that neutrals in time of war could carry only the goods that they had carried during time of peace. Between this rule and Napoleon's Berlin decree attempting to blockade Britain, the end of our lucrative expansion was near.

[2] The terms of trade (net barter) are obtained by dividing a price index of imports into a price index of exports.

Jefferson, fearing that if we continued our shipping we would become involved in the war, declared an embargo which was followed by the precipitous decline observed in 1808. Shipping and trade then partially recovered between 1809 and 1812, although never completely, nor to the level of prosperity enjoyed before 1807. Then, with America's actual entry into the conflict in 1812, the British blockade effectively eliminated most of our external trade until the end of that war.

There can be no doubt that the years 1793 through 1807 were extraordinarily prosperous ones for the American economy. The fact appears in the numerous literary descriptions by people who observed the economy during that time and in the few figures that

CHART 14.   U.S. TERMS OF TRADE, 1790-1815
(Base 1790)

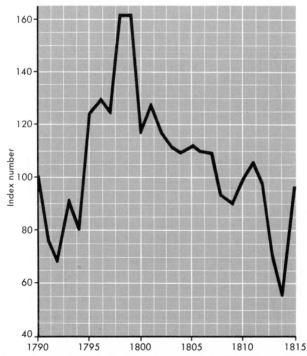

Source: Douglass C. North, *The Economic Growth of the United States, 1790-1860,* p. 31.

we do have—such as urbanization increasing from 5 to 7.3 per cent and rapid expansion of the major cities (Baltimore, Boston, New York, and Philadelphia) between 1790 and 1810. There can also be little doubt that the period between 1793 and 1808 was one of full employment, in which our resources were utilized completely. A substantial increase in productivity resulted particularly from the growth in size of the domestic market. That growth, in turn, was stimulated as the high prices being paid for our exports attracted America's agricultural products into the marketplace and made it possible for farmers to specialize in producing, thereby pulling them out of self-sufficiency and into the market economy. Moreover, the temporary phenomenon of very high export prices coupled with very low import prices (reflecting the situation of a world at war) meant that we became better off, at least for this very brief period, as a result of being able to buy more manufactured imports with every dollar of exports than we had ever bought before.[3]

With the embargo, this prosperity came to an end, and the year 1808 was characterized by depression and unemployment that reached the seacoast and the market-oriented sectors of the American economy. Despite some relaxation of the embargo, with subsequent acts designed to stimulate trade with one or another of the belligerents, we never completely recovered in the years 1808 to 1812, and a good deal of the capital that businessmen had invested in shipping now turned instead into manufacturing. The embargo meant not merely that we did not sell to belligerents—we could not buy from them. As a result, the prices of manufactured goods rose dramatically, encouraging businessmen to put their capital where the profits were. Consequently, where before 1808 only 15 cotton mills had been built in the United States, by the end of 1809 there were 87 additional mills, and this expansion continued right up through the War of 1812. Similar activity spread far afield into manufacturing a variety of other kinds of goods formerly imported.

It is clear that American capital would at that time have been

---

[3] It should be noted, however, that favorable terms of trade do not necessarily imply any improvement in the income position of a country. This was an extraordinary situation.

more profitably employed, however, if it could have been used in shipping and the earnings from that shipping then used to buy British manufactures. The British had greater supplies of capital and skilled labor to produce goods more efficiently and cheaply than we could. By the same token, we enjoyed advantages in shipping. The embargo, therefore, had forced us for a time into an inefficient course. American manufacturing developed prematurely, thriving only under the artificial protection of the embargo and the war. When the War of 1812 ended, England's more efficient exports were shattering competition that brought about a drastic decline in American manufacturing.

Even during the years 1808 to 1814, the economy was less prosperous with this more inefficient orientation of production than it had been in the booming period prior to the embargo. Not only were our resources employed less efficiently between 1808 and 1814; for a time there was substantial unemployment, and eventually we became involved in a war, with all that meant in terms of dislocation of economic activity in the United States.

INDUSTRIALIZATION AND WELFARE

There has been a widely held view that in the course of industrialization the well-being of the wage earner has fallen. Debate has long raged over this topic, but not until recently has the weight of evidence suggested that in England this was not really so.[4] In the U.S., in support of the argument that our per capita income fell during the Industrial Revolution (the 1830's and 1840's being a period of substantial industrialization), a set of statistics is widely quoted.[5] Per capita income adjusted for changes in the price level is shown to be higher in 1799 than it was again until 1849.[6] The figure falls slightly between 1799 and substantially in the next

[4] See Max Hartwell, "The Rising Standard of Living in England, 1800-1850," *EHR*, 2d ser., XIII, No. 3 (April 1961).

[5] Robert F. Martin, *National Income in the United States, 1799 to 1938* (New York: National Industrial Conference Board, 1939).

[6] A fall in real wages and a fall in per capita income are not the same thing. National income is made up of both wages and property income (profits, interest, and rent). Real wages could fall either because income was falling or because of a redistribution of income from wages to property income.

decade, showing no striking rise until 1839. It does not exceed the figure of 1799 until half a century later. More recently, George Taylor [7] suggested that agricultural settlement in New England and movement to the West was unfavorable to productivity increase before 1840. While the main emphasis of Taylor's analysis is upon diminishing returns (and therefore declining productivity) in eastern agriculture and a relatively inefficient agriculture in the West, the burden of his analysis is that per capita income increased only slowly before 1840.

Martin's methods and figures have been roundly criticized by experts on the subject.[8] Moreover, I doubt that one can draw the conclusion that productivity did not increase substantially before 1840. If we assume that a worker in agriculture was half as productive as one in nonagricultural pursuits, then it would have taken a 22 per cent decrease in agricultural productivity to counteract the shift of workers from agricultural to nonagricultural pursuits (and a 50 per cent decrease if we allow for increases in the percentage of the population engaged in gainful employment). Such a fall is simply unreasonable, since we have reason to believe that in the major agricultural crops of corn and cotton there is evidence of increasing productivity during this period.[9] Our fragmentary figures on productivity growth in manufacturing also indicate that there was substantial gain. Indeed, everything we know about the economy suggests that in terms of technological change, the growing size of the market, and improving human skills, it must have been a period of rising per capita income.

The weight of evidence is therefore against lowered per capita income, except for one curious fact: in 1799 per capita incomes were extraordinary and may have been almost as high as they were half a century later. Note, however, that our explanation of

[7] *Economic Change in the Civil War Era*, ed. David T. Gilchrist and W. Davis Lewis (Greenville, Del.: Eleutherian Mills–Hagley Foundation, 1965).

[8] "National Income Estimates for the Period Prior to 1870," *Income and Wealth of the United States, Trends and Structure*, ed. Simon S. Kuznets (Cambridge: Eng. Bowes & Bowes, 1952); and William N. Parker and Franklee Whartenby, "The Growth of Output before 1840," *Trends in the American Economy in the Nineteenth Century*, Studies in Income and Wealth, XXIV (Princeton, N.J.: published for NBER by Princeton Univ., 1960).

[9] For a further discussion of these issues, see Douglass C. North, *EDCC*, IX (April 1961).

this fact differs from Martin's. We are looking at the period (1793 to 1807) as a peculiar one, constituting a bulge in the over-all long-run pattern of American growth induced by the phenomenon of the new nation taking advantage of a world at war and earning very substantial income from exports, re-exports, and shipping. The following chart (Chart 15) shows per capita credit from the balance of payments growing from only $7.00 per capita, which we noted in an earlier chapter, to almost $24.00 per capita in 1807 and then falling back again by 1815 to a level of around $8.00 to $9.00 per capita. In short, this atypical period was one that produced a very

CHART 15.   PER CAPITA CREDITS IN BALANCE OF PAYMENTS, 1790-1815

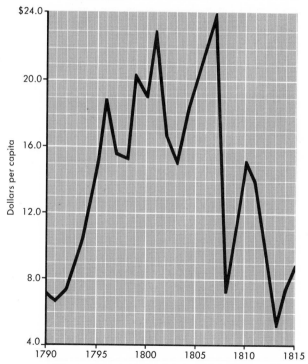

Source: Douglass C. North, "Early National Income Estimates of the U.S.," *EDCC*, IX, No. 3 (April 1961), 390.

brief period of unparalleled prosperity. It was followed by a period of reorganization after the second war with England—a reorganization made painful by the readjustment out of manufacturing—and thereafter by sustained expansion. If properly interpreted, the figures of Martin are on extraordinarily shaky ground—first of all in terms of the methods; second, in the light of the evidence advanced above, the interpretation suggested is very different from a view of declining welfare during an industrial revolution. Evidence suggests that our productivity was growing all through the first fifty years of the nineteenth century, but that in the very early period of 1793 to 1807 we experienced an unusual bulge as a result of peculiar events that lasted for a very short time.[10]

[10] The unusually large per capita credits in the balance of payments would still not account for a bulge in income that would equal Martin's figure of 1799 as compared with his figures for the next three decades.

chapter 6

ACCELERATION OF
U. S. ECONOMIC GROWTH,
1815-1860

In taking a long look at the American economy up until 1815, we have seen it emerge from Colonial status, struggle through a period of turmoil with Confederation, and then enjoy an era of prosperity and economic growth as the new nation took advantage of neutrality in a world at war—until it, too, was drawn into the conflict and an inconclusive war. Somewhere during the period between 1815 and 1860, the rate of growth of the American economy accelerated. There is no complete explanation of precisely how it happened. What this chapter attempts is some fitting together of the pieces of the puzzle, some weighing of the evidence.

When America emerged in 1815 from the second war with England, its position was somewhat analogous to that of 1790. This was still a small newcomer among the nations of the world. Although its population had increased from not quite 4,000,000 in 1790 to about 8,400,000 in 1815, the citizenry was scattered over a vast area; approximately half lived in the North and half in the South, although by now a substantial total of more than one million adventurous souls had moved across the Appalachian Mountains and settled in the New West. Many of these had come in the wake of the Lewis and Clark expedition of 1803, which gave evidence of untold prospects for new settlement and development in the lands acquired from the French in the Louisiana Purchase at the beginning of the nineteenth century. While the vast, promising, unsettled reaches of the West now added a potential asset of unknown value to the scattered settlement up and down the coast of the United States, another aspect of the economy had changed little since 1790. This was our relationship to foreign countries. By and large, the things we did best—shipping and exports of our agricultural commodities—were circumscribed by the navigation laws and by the mercantilist policies that still dominated most of Europe. Our international trade seemed to be reverting to the kind of dilemma faced in 1790; however, there was one significant difference—cotton. When Eli Whitney invented the cotton gin in 1793, he changed the face of the South. His innovation became the mainspring of the southern economy, insured the perpetuation of slavery, and ultimately helped to promote the conflict that was to engulf America in 1861. Cotton rapidly took over from every other commodity in the South wherever its planting was feasible, so that the once rather diversified southern agriculture now became concentrated on cotton production in most areas. Two exceptions were South Carolina, where rice was still of major importance, and Louisiana, with its sugar cane.[1] But cotton made the big difference in the economy after 1815, ruling as king in the South and exerting an important influence in the national pattern of development.

Before we look at the pattern of interregional dependence that developed from such southern specialization, we should recall that Jefferson's embargo sent a good part of dispossessed American capital and resources into manufacturing. Production of cotton textiles, machinery, and equipment expanded so rapidly in America between 1808 and 1814 that many people were optimistically contemplating industrialization as an accomplished fact. We know now that a peacetime economy revealed our inadequacies. Bankruptcies spread as English textiles and other manufactured products flooded into the United States and effectively undersold the higher-cost manufactures produced locally. Clearly, America lacked British

---

[1] Cotton, rice, and sugar became the major cash crops for sale outside the region; however, it is well to remember that the South continued to produce substantial amounts of corn, oats, and other agricultural products, too.

manufacturing efficiency and was not yet ready to claim any birthright as a manufacturing nation. With some few exceptions (such as the Waltham Mills, to be discussed later) this was a period of readjustment for American industry.

Following the second war with England, the separate regions of the United States became more specialized, as they concentrated on producing commodities and interchanging with each other in a way that was to become a mainstay of extensive development. The earliest days of this interregional and international trade found the South trading in cotton with England. Britain at this time was in the midst of the Industrial Revolution, and the prime products of the new factory system were vast quantities of textiles. A growing demand for cotton logically resulted, and this demand America, more pre-eminently than any other country in the world, was able to meet. Whenever supply did not keep pace with demand, cotton prices soared, and planters were induced to put more of their acreage into cotton. As the South exported cotton to England (and to a lesser extent to France), it bought, in turn, all its needed goods. Among these were food supplies to maintain the plantation, including its slaves; manufactured goods to equip the plantation; also insurance and shipping services. The foodstuffs were in part indigenous, but a more detailed look indicates that the South was only partially self-sufficient and that it also depended upon the West. From there came corn, wheat, and the livestock products that were in growing demand on the plantation, so that as the plantation way of life expanded in the South (particularly in the new South —Louisiana and Mississippi—which was highly concentrated in cotton and to a lesser extent in sugar production), the growing need for foodstuffs for these areas was met by the West, along the newly developing artery of the Mississippi River. This large-scale trade became possible when the advent of the steamboat on the Mississippi in 1816 assured that not only could goods be floated downriver but that paddlewheelers could beat their way back up against the current with goods for the new West. Such interchange accounts for the ties between the West and the South.[2]

[2] A major unresolved issue is the extent to which the South depended upon the West for foodstuffs. The statistics (particularly before 1840) are incomplete. It may be that a good part of the trade from the West down the

At that date, the Northeast was primarily engaged in shipping, commerce, and insurance; and these services, too, were in demand by southern planters. Increasingly, the Northeast was also discovering larger southern and western markets for its manufactures. Burgeoning trade, population, and incomes in the South and West were creating greater demands for domestic manufactures, making it feasible for the Northeast to produce on a larger scale, a basis more competitive with imports.[3] A flexible pattern of trade had now been established. At first, income from the South flowed both to the West for foodstuffs and to the Northeast for services, insurance, and shipping. Then manufacturing also began to draw southern funds to the Northeast, and the pattern became more intricate as the Northeast, increasingly engaged in manufactures, came to need more foodstuffs to nourish its industrial population. At this point, the West became oriented to providing agricultural goods to the Northeast, and even to Europe, rather than just to the South. This pattern of international and especially interregional trade was the pivot on which America's economy swung during the period 1815 to 1860.

To discover why the pattern developed requires a look in more detail at each of the separate regions. It was the behavior of prices that decided the way southern development was to take place, and Chart 16 fortifies this view. It shows, on the one hand, the prices of cotton and, on the other, the sales of lands in the new Southwest (Arkansas, Louisiana, Mississippi, Alabama) and Florida.

Mississippi River went by ship to the East or was exported, rather than providing food for the plantation. It is reasonable to assume that in periods of low cotton prices planters put more acreage into corn in order to be self-sufficient, because cotton was not as profitable, whereas in periods of high cotton prices they devoted all possible acreage to cotton and bought their corn and other foodstuffs from the West. However, only the development of careful *annual* statistical data of food purchases in the *New South* (since there is no argument that the Old South tended to become more self-sufficient) will settle the issue.

[3] The importance of early tariff legislation in the revival of manufacturing has been a much debated subject. The Acts of 1816, 1824, and 1828 all provided protection and with the fall in prices after 1818 were probably important in the revival of some branches of the textile industry; but by 1830 the U.S. was exporting textiles and was able to stand on its own feet. In addition, the high transport costs into the interior provided protection for the early iron industry in western Pennsylvania between 1820 and 1837.

Note the coincidence between periods of high prices and periods of surging migration into new lands in the Southwest. In each of these periods, higher prices for agricultural commodities (in this case, cotton) caused planters with their slaves to move into the new, rich, fertile land of the Southwest in quest of such rewards for increasing the supply of cotton. (The same pattern applied later to the West, with different kinds of commodities.) Therefore, the expansion in the South over this period was induced by the growing demand for cotton in Europe, leading to rising prices, to surges of expansion into the new Southwest, and to an ever-increasing supply of cotton. The British helped to finance this expansion into

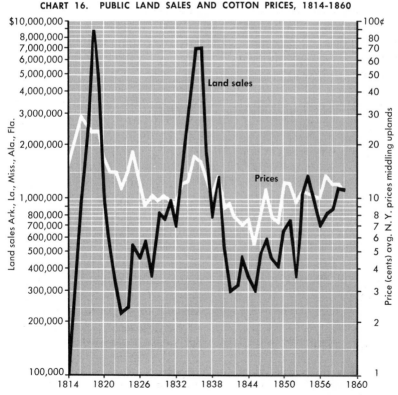

CHART 16. PUBLIC LAND SALES AND COTTON PRICES, 1814-1860

Source: Douglass C. North, *The Economic Growth of the United States, 1790-1860,* p. 124.

new cotton land by making loans to banks in Louisiana and Mississippi whose funds, in turn, were used to finance planters in expansion and the opening up of these new lands.

Although early western settlement had occurred soon after the Revolutionary War, what really inaugurated a change in its status was the opening of a far-reaching transportation network. The first link of this was forged from the interconnected rivers that bound together the Mississippi, the Missouri, and the Ohio; by this route, the products of the West could flow to the South. Later, additional canals opened farther parts of the West and, even more importantly, connected the whole region with the East Coast—again in part financed by British capital.

The West was able to produce profitably both cereals and commodities that depended upon cereals. Wheat, corn, and livestock products were the mainstays of the western economy and the major items shipped to the South.[4] As decades wore on and better transport facilities were available, a growing demand expanded the movement of these goods into the East itself.

The West, however, was more diversified than the South. For example, lead was early found in Missouri, and a substantial downriver trade developed as ore was floated down to New Orleans and exported. Similarly, copper in Michigan and iron ore in western Pennsylvania produced early patterns of mining activity, and the iron industry itself flourished in western Pennsylvania, southern Ohio, and northern Kentucky. So while the South concentrated with single-minded attention on its cotton production, the West early reached out into more diversified economic activity.

A look at Chart 17, where wheat and corn prices are compared with sales of land in seven western states, shows a familiar pattern emerging. As with southern cotton, so with western wheat, rising prices induced mass movement into new lands. In the West, the expansion was into the rich lands of Ohio, Illinois, Indiana, Michigan, Iowa, Wisconsin, and Missouri. Output of western agricultural goods responded to price increases induced by the growing demand from the East and later (beginning with the Irish famine in

---

[4] Note, however, footnote 2, which suggests the possibility that western foodstuffs may also have been going to the East or have been exported as well in this early period.

CHART 17.   LAND SALES IN SEVEN WESTERN STATES, 1815-1860

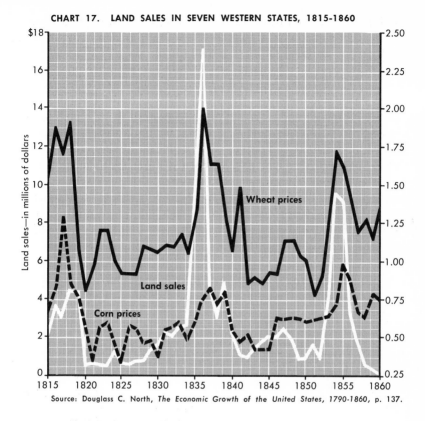

Source: Douglass C. North, *The Economic Growth of the United States, 1790-1860*, p. 137.

1844-1846) from Europe. With an expanding transportation network, the West was able to realize its potential in a pattern of
interregional trade based on market-oriented production. Parenthe-
tically, the West—already more diversified than the South—was
destined to become a more broadly based economy and one in which
manufacturing would later develop.

In 1820, the Northeast was just recovering from its abortive
industrialization, induced by British competition. The area was still
dependent upon commerce, shipping, and agriculture during this
period; in fact, even though relatively declining in significance, the
shipping and commerce sector continued to be an important source

of income and well-being in the Northwest all through the nineteenth century. This was especially true in the period between 1815 and 1860. American ships and their goods were trading all over the world, and merchants of Boston, Salem, and other ports along the East Coast were dominant in trade in every part of the globe, from China and India to Africa and to all parts of Europe. Agriculture, fishing, and even whaling continued in the nineteenth century to hold a place of importance in the Northeast economy.

But the most interesting and significant development in the period between 1815 and 1860 was first the gradual, then the dramatically vigorous revival of manufacturing. It began with a slow stirring in the 1820's (although much more strongly in Massachusetts than elsewhere); then, in the 1830's, manufacturing—particularly of cotton textiles—rapidly gained momentum all through New England, in New York, and to a lesser extent in Pennsylvania. Coincident with the growth of textiles, the iron industry, machinery production, and a variety of other manufactures also evolved during this period, reflecting the beginning of a diversified manu-

TABLE 8. LEADING BRANCHES OF MANUFACTURE IN THE UNITED STATES, 1860

Item	Employment	Value of product (000's of $)	Value added by manufacture (000's of $)	Rank by value added
1. Flour and meal	27,682	$248,580	$40,083	4
2. Cotton goods	114,955	107,338	54,671	1
3. Lumber	75,595	104,928	53,570	2
4. Boots and shoes	123,026	91,889	49,161	3
5. Men's clothing	114,800	80,831	36,681	5
6. Iron (cast, forged, rolled, wrought)	48,975	73,175	35,689	6
7. Leather	22,679	67,306	22,786	9
8. Woolen goods	40,597	60,685	25,030	8
9. Liquors	12,706	56,589	21,667	10
10. Machinery	41,223	52,010	32,566	7

Source: U.S. Census Bureau, *Eighth Census of the United States, 1860, Manufactures* (Washington: GPO, 1865), pp. 733-42.

facturing activity. The ten leading types of manufacturing in America in 1860 are shown in Table 8. These are essentially of two kinds, one being oriented to resource industries—that is, dealing in the processing of resources such as the production of flour and cornmeal from wheat and corn. This substantial part of northeastern manufacturing typically developed at geographical locations where grain from the farms was brought for transshipment. Lumbering was another important resource-oriented industry.

The second group of manufactures that had evolved by 1860 comprised light manufacturing. Cotton goods stands out in the data; so do boots and shoes, men's clothing, leather, and woolen goods; and machinery is destined for still further future expansion. A rather broad pattern of manufacturing had evolved in the North- east by 1860, with cotton textiles in the vanguard. A pioneer in this industry, the Waltham Mills, was established in 1813 in Massa- chusetts during the second war with England. The flood of English textiles that followed the peace treaty of the following year did not bankrupt the Waltham Mills, as it did many other textile firms. Their success stemmed primarily from large-scale production, coupled with production of what was called a coarse sheeting, a cheap and simple cotton cloth that a frontier, pioneering society could put to use in all kinds of finished cotton textile goods. In addition, the English power loom was adapted to American needs and put to work in the Waltham Mills (foreshadowing the con- tinuous modification of British technology to fit American condi- tions). Thus with low-grade cotton fabric being produced by efficient technology and on a large scale, there was put together a mill that even during the years 1816 to 1819 managed to survive and actually do rather well. While this was an exceptional case, the underlying conditions favorable to manufacturing expansion were gradually changing. One element had not changed: labor and capital were still in relatively short supply in this country and were therefore more costly. Wages were very high compared to those in England, and capital was more expensive. Early manufacturing had to find some offset for the high cost of these two largest ingredients if it wished to compete. As in the case of Waltham Mills, one workable approach proved to be the adaptation and modification of British machinery and equipment, so that it fitted our particular needs and characteristics. Progress was made whenever a machine could be devised to economize on high-priced labor by utilizing richly abundant natural resources such as waterpower. It was this ability to innovate and to modify the British improvement, coupled with the growing size of the American market, which reduced our manufacturing costs compared to England's. The mills and factories could now begin to produce on a large enough and efficient enough scale to compete with foreign imports.

To return to the question that began this chapter—what accelerated growth in the American economy between 1815 and 1860? —and to fit together some of the pieces of an answer, we must first observe that industrialization in the Northeast, though important, cannot claim full credit. In fact, it is clear that all three major regions contributed. In both the West and the South, incomes rose with more efficient agriculture and with migration into new and richer lands. In the West, a growing market orientation led to greater specialization and division of labor. Whatever may be thought of an economy based on slavery, there is no doubt that income in the South was rising too, that cotton production was growing apace, and that as a result there was also development there. It was the whole American economy that was responsible for the accelerated growth, since productive efficiency was increasing in each region.

In terms of the characteristics discussed earlier as determinants of productivity change, investment in skills and knowledge played an important role. Skilled engineers, craftsmen, and technicians— not, in those days, formally educated men, but graduates of the Yankee schools of experience—came forward to adapt and modify the techniques of Britain for American use; ingenious craftsmen, carpenters, and mechanics were the people who typically made the significant innovations. Formal education, too, was comparatively common. Table 9 shows the ratio of students to total population in the United States and in New England, compared with other parts of the world. Human capital also provided the essential skilled labor force that was so important for high levels of productivity in both manufacturing and agriculture. The second factor, technology, includes some indigenous innovations like the cotton gin of Eli Whitney, which transformed a whole region, as well as the prosaic sewing machine, which played an important role in the industrial economy. Finally, increasing efficiency of organization was im-

TABLE 9. INTERNATIONAL COMPARISON OF RELATIVE SCHOOL
POPULATIONS, 1850

	Ratio of students to total population
New England	25.71
Denmark	21.73
U.S. (excluding slaves)	20.40
Sweden	17.85
Saxony	16.66
Prussia	16.12
Norway	14.28
Belgium	12.04
Great Britain (on the books)	11.76
Great Britain (in attendance Mar. 31, 1851)	14.28
France	9.52
Austria	7.29
Holland	6.99
Ireland	6.89
Greece	5.55
Russia	2.00
Portugal	1.22

Source: U.S. Census Bureau, A Compendium of the Seventh Census, J. D. B. DeBow, Supt. of Census (Washington, 1854), p. 148.

portant and is really a central theme of this chapter. Regional specialization and the growth of interregional trade encouraged the shift out of self-sufficiency into the market economy (with resulting improvements in efficiency), created larger markets, so that economies of scale were achieved, and encouraged the improvement in factor and product markets.

INDUSTRIALIZATION AND ECONOMIC GROWTH

Economic historians tend to identify economic growth with industrialization. Despite the evidence that some nonindustrial countries such as Denmark and New Zealand have achieved high levels of income, economic historians have followed the traditional line of preoccupation with England's Industrial Revolution in viewing economic growth as synonymous with industrialization. Much of the economic history of the world has been written in terms of the development of "preconditions" for industrialization and then a description of the development of manufacturing. This view has been formalized and popularized by Walt Rostow in a book entitled *The Stages of Economic Growth* [5] which attempts to put this long-accepted view into a theoretical set of stages. The most important stage for our purposes here is the stage entitled "The Take-Off" into self-sustained economic growth; and as Rostow points out, the take-off is really a return to an old-fashioned notion about industrialization. Rostow describes the take-off as a brief interval of two or three decades during which the economy develops growth in a more or less automatic fashion. The three specific conditions essential to the take-off are (1) a rise in the rate of capital formation from, say, 5 or fewer per cent to 10 per cent or more of national income or net national product; (2) the development of one or more substantial manufacturing sectors of a high rate of growth; and (3) the existence or quick emergence of a political, social, and institutional framework which exploits this impetus to expansion.

He suggests that the critical dates for the United States are between 1843 and 1860; that a major source of the increase in the rate of capital formation came from foreign borrowing, particularly from Britain; and that the leading sector which characterized and led this whole development was railroad expansion in the East in the 1840's and in the West in the 1850's. The railroad was the leading sector and was the critical factor in this process—first of all, because it lowered the cost of transportation; second, because it induced the growth of other manufacturing sectors as a result of the demand for iron, for machinery, and for lumber in the whole process of railroad construction; and third, because it permitted the development of new export sectors which in turn financed the import of capital goods.

Available statistical evidence lends no support to this hypothesis whatsoever. First, there is no evidence that the rate of capital formation increased from 5 to 10 per cent during this period.

[5] W.W. Rostow, *The Stages of Economic Growth: A Non-Communist Manifesto* (Cambridge: Cambridge Univ., 1960).

Foreign borrowing was nonexistent in the 1840's—in fact, just the reverse. We were repatriating securities to Britain in the wake of a severe depression. It was not until the end of the decade that we again began borrowing, and the amount of that borrowing all through the 1850's was modest indeed—a far smaller proportion of national product than it had been in the 1830's. Moreover, it is perfectly clear that the export of gold as a result of gold discoveries in California provided far more credit in the U.S. balance of payments for import of capital goods than did foreign borrowing.

Second, while the railroad clearly did lower transport costs as suggested in Chapter 9, it was not such a drastic reduction as the economic historian has traditionally viewed it. With respect to the railroad's inducing expansion in other sectors of manufacturing, the recent research by Robert Fogel on this subject suggests that the demand for railroad iron in the decade ending 1849 was 10 per cent of the consumption of domestic crude iron. The demand for other products was equally a small percentage of the total demand for those commodities. It is perfectly clear therefore that the railroad demand was not an important or crucial factor in the expansion of those industries.

Finally, Rostow presumably had in mind, by the opening up of new exports, the grain trade in which we developed exports of grain in the 1840's and 1850's. The exports of grain for the Irish famine in the middle of the 1840's took place before the railroad had penetrated the West, and both in the 1840's and in the 1850's the exports of grain went primarily by water and not by railroad. Moreover, wheat and grain stuffs never comprised more than 15 per cent of total exports by five-year average, in contrast to cotton, which continued to dominate our exports and claimed more than 50 per cent of the total. Cotton exports also, by and large, moved from the plantation to the export points by water.

The case of the United States lends no support to the Rostow hypothesis, nor does that of any other country. Simon Kuznets concludes (in a paper presented at the International Economic Association meetings in 1960, which was on the subject of the take-off):

Unless I have completely misunderstood Professor Rostow's definition of take-off and its statistical characteristics, I can only conclude the available evidence lends no support to Professor Rostow's suggestion.[6]

Even more important than the empirical shortcomings of Rostow's stages are the theoretical shortcomings. Rostow's stages really are not a theory, in the sense of offering a dynamic model of change in which we can see how the United States moved from one stage to the next. As a result, his set of stages falls far short of the promise which he offers in his statements about this work.

Furthermore, his take-off is not only a return to the old-fashioned view that industrialization is synonymous with economic growth but also is a return to the old-fashioned view that capital as narrowly defined is the critical factor in economic growth. Yet, as noted in Chapter 1, additions to the capital stock appear to account for only a very small proportion of our increases in productivity over time. This appears to be what Rostow had in mind in his discussion of capital.[7] If, in Rostow's view, capital had a strategic role to play because it embodied new technological advance, then it is not apparent why we need such a rise in the rate of capital formation. All that is needed is the capital to replace machinery and equipment—that is, gross capital formation which will embody new technological knowledge—but this does not necessarily imply a rise in the rate of net capital formation. As a matter of fact, however, it is probably capital broadly conceived to include human investment as well as physical investment that is the proper criterion, and this does not figure at all in Rostow's scheme.

Finally, there is a great deal of confusion about the significance of leading sectors' inducing investments in other kinds of manufacturing and enterprise. This is not necessarily a gain to the economy over and above what is already reflected in the declining costs of the "leading sector." For example, in the case of railroads, a fall in transportation costs reflects the total improvements of productivity of both railroads and of the other industries that supplied parts and whose expansion was induced by the railroad. It is double-

[6] Simon S. Kuznets, "Notes on the Take-off," *The Economics of Take-Off into Sustained Growth*, W.W. Rostow, ed., proceedings of an International Economic Association Conference, 1960 (New York: St. Martin's Press, 1964).

[7] For evidence, see Steven Enke, *Economics for Development* (Englewood Cliffs, N.J.: Prentice-Hall, 1963), p. 198.

counting to count also the gains that may accrue in productivity from the industries that go into railroad transportation services. There is an additional gain in efficiency *only* if the market for the products of these industries was not big enough for them to produce at the most efficient scale before the railroad came along to increase the demand for this product and thereby to lower their costs of production. Only then would there be lower costs to all the other users of that industry, and thereby an additional gain to society.

chapter 7

THE ECONOMY
OF THE
ANTEBELLUM SOUTH

In the years preceding the Civil War, the South was heavily dependent upon the concentrated production of a few staple commodities for markets outside the region. Cotton was by far the most important—although rice in South Carolina, sugar in Louisiana, and tobacco in the upper parts of the South were also significant export commodities. The plantation economy that characterized the production of these goods employed large amounts of land in complementary use with large amounts of labor; in the new South, accordingly, the size of the plantation was substantial. The supply of labor was, of course, slaves. They were the major capital investment in the plantation system. Between 1802 and 1860, the price of a prime field hand rose from about $600 at the earlier date to $1,800 by the time of the Civil War. This increase in slave prices was a rational reflection of their value in commodity production. A salient feature of the southern system was the availability of rich land to the west for extensive expansion of cotton culture; and between 1815 and 1860, planters and slaves moved westward in a series of surges that led to rapid population growth of the new Southwest. Table 10 shows the increase in free and slave population in these new states. The main surges into the Southwest occurred between 1816 and 1819 and between 1833 and 1837, although there was some expansion in land sales in the latter part of the 1850's, of much more modest proportions. There were several important differences between the plantations of the older areas of the Carolinas and Georgia in contrast with those of the new Southwest. Plantations of the older areas had higher production costs of cotton and on the whole were less specialized, whereas the new plantations —particularly in Louisiana and Mississippi—tended to be highly concentrated in large-scale production of cotton or sugar.

Despite the fact that we think of the South in terms of a plantation economy, the majority of southern whites did not own slaves. A very high proportion of them lived on small farms and were only peripherally related to the market. As a matter of fact, a characteristic of the South was that a large part of its population was neither regularly involved in the sale of goods to the market nor attracted into market production during these years. With the expansion of economic opportunity in the Southwest, farmers of the Old South tended to migrate, but there was less tendency for development of local markets in the old area itself. Another striking characteristic of the South in the antebellum period was its lack of urbanization. Aside from the growth of a few ports to implement the cotton trade—such as Mobile, Savannah, Charleston, and New Orleans—there were few cities of any size. New Orleans alone gave every indication of a thriving and growing city. In 1860 it was the only southern city among the country's top 15 in population. Along with this absence of urbanization was a lack of locally oriented industries and services, conspicuously fewer in the South than elsewhere on a per capita basis. Even retail trade, most rudimentary of such services, was less than in any other area in the country. Some of these characteristics have led historians to the belief that the South was a stagnating economy, but the evidence does not support this contention. It is true that per capita income in the South Atlantic and East South Central states was below the national average; but in the West South Central area the per capita income was substantially higher than the national average in 1840 and even in 1860 (Table 11). Moreover, the trend in income in the South suggests that the per capita income—far from being stagnant—was growing during this period at a rate approximately equal to the national average. A final characteristic of the southern economy,

TABLE 10. POPULATION OF FREE (NEGRO AND WHITE) AND SLAVES OF

Year	Alabama		Arkansas		Florida	
	F	S	F	S	F	S
1820	86,622	41,879	12,638	1,617	——	——
1830	191,978	117,549	25,812	4,576	19,229	15,501
1840	337,224	253,532	77,639	19,935	28,760	25,717
1850	428,779	342,892	162,797	47,100	48,135	39,309
1860	529,121	435,080	324,335	111,115	78,680	61,745

Source: U.S. Congress, House, *Preliminary Report on the Eighth Census, 1860* (Washington:

important for our analysis, is that investment in human capital for education was conspicuously lower in the South than elsewhere in the United States. The ratio of pupils to white population in 1840 was 5.72 per cent in slaveholding states compared to 18.41 per cent in nonslaveholding states. Illiteracy as a percentage of the white population was 7.46 in the slaveholding states and only 2.13 per cent in the nonslaveholding states, despite the substantial numbers of illiterate immigrants who were entering the country in the North. The slaveholding states in 1850 had only slightly less than half of the white population of the northern states; nevertheless, they had less than one third as many public schools, one fourth as many pupils, one twentieth of the public libraries, one sixth as many volumes in these libraries. Admittedly, the South was conspicuously lower in terms of its investment in the education of its white people than was the rest of the United States in these years before the Civil War.

From this very brief and summary description can be drawn some important analytical conclusions about the South. The first is an obvious one: the comparative advantage of cotton over alternative forms of production was so great that this was the rational investment for the southerner to make. In the few years around 1845, cotton's fall to 5 cents per pound was viewed as a temporary period of very low prices and not a permanent one. With this ex-

ALABAMA, ARKANSAS, FLORIDA, LOUISIANA, AND MISSISSIPPI, 1820-1860

| Louisiana | | Mississippi | | Total |
F	S	F	S	(F and S)
83,857	69,064	42,634	32,814	371,125
106,251	109,588	70,962	65,659	727,105
183,959	168,452	180,440	195,211	1,470,869
272,953	244,809	296,698	309,878	2,193,300
376,276	331,726	354,674	436,631	3,093,383

GPO, 1862), pp. 126-33.

ception, the southerner felt—and rightly so—that his income was higher by remaining in cotton than it would have been had he devoted his slaves, his land, and his other resources to any other type of economic activity. Second, all the characteristics of the southern picture indicate a profit-maximizing economy in which people acted rationally. The whole process of the new land entries during that period was one in which increasing profitability of cotton, as a result of rising prices, led to the waves of westward movement described in Chapter 6.[1] High cotton prices resulted in surges of land sales in the new Southwest, to take advantage of the activity. Indeed, this points up an important factor in our whole expansion westward: the process was induced by the rising profitability of producing commodities that were in demand in the rest of the United States and in the world beyond.

The behavior of cotton prices shown in Chart 16 (Chapter 6) was the result of the following sequence of events. A period of high cotton prices led to a surge of planters and slaves into the new Southwest. For a period of three to four years, land was cleared, a preliminary crop of corn was sometimes planted; then, when the land was ready, cotton was planted, and a substantial increase in the supply of cotton took place. The result was to lower the price of cotton drastically, with the result that it no longer in-

[1] See Chart 16 in Chapter 6.

duced further westward expansion, and some new lands were planted in corn. Cotton prices tended to remain low for a rather lengthy period, however, because any increase in demand was met by a further increase in supply, since planters who had cleared the land could shift from corn back to cotton again if it became more profitable to do so. This continued until demand had increased enough to employ all the cleared land, then rising prices again ensued. The relationship between corn and cotton here is important. As noted above, in periods of very low prices it paid the planter to produce his own foodstuff to feed his plantation slaves; but when the price of cotton rose, then it was more profitable to plow under the corn, to specialize in producing cotton, and to buy his corn and other foodstuffs from the West. A somewhat different situation existed in the Old South where cotton tended to be somewhat less profitable; this led to more diversification and to the production of corn alongside cotton, to approach a self-sufficient plantation.

The lack of urbanization and locally oriented industry and trade in the South probably reflected two characteristics of the southern

TABLE 11. PERSONAL INCOME PER CAPITA IN EACH REGION AS PERCENTAGE OF UNITED STATES AVERAGE, 1840-1950 (U.S. = 100)

Regions	1840	1860	1880	1900	1920	1930	1940	1950
NORTHEAST	135	139	141	137	132	138	124	115
New England	132	143	141	134	124	129	121	109
Mid. Atlantic	136	137	141	139	134	140	124	116
NORTH CENTRAL	68	68	98	103	100	101	103	106
E. No. Central	67	69	102	106	108	111	112	112
W. No. Central	75	66	90	97	87	82	84	94
SOUTH	76	72	51	51	62	55	65	73
So. Atlantic	70	65	45	45	59	56	69	74
E. So. Central	73	68	51	49	52	48	55	62
W. So. Central	144	115	60	61	72	61	70	80
WEST			190	163	122	115	125	114
Mountain			168	139	100	83	92	96
Pacific			204	163	135	130	138	121

For footnoted details, see source: Richard A. Easterlin, "Regional Income Trends, 1840-1950," *American Economic History*, Seymour E. Harris, ed. (New York: McGraw-Hill Book Company, 1961), p. 528.

economy. First, cotton production did not encourage additional kinds of economic activity, industry, or commerce. The planter had only to get his baled cotton to the wharf of one of the abundant waterways that proliferated in the South; from there the crop could be shipped out, and there, in turn, he could receive whatever imports he wanted. Indeed, the planter was relieved of any economic activity other than raising cotton itself by the factor system, under which the New England or the English merchant bought the cotton, provided the imported goods for the planter, and carried on all necessary shipping and insurance services. The second characteristic of the South, which probably inhibited more diversified activities, was the distribution of income. This was obviously very unequal, with most of the labor force enslaved. The planter who was well-to-do tended to buy imported goods or to send his children north to school, but he used few goods that would encourage local industry in the South. As for the rest of the populace, they had such low incomes and were to such a large extent self-sufficient that they could not encourage the growth of locally oriented goods and services.

Still, there is nothing about either the crop characteristics or the income picture of the South that suggests an economy that was not viable or, indeed, thriving. Slavery formed the base of an economy that achieved substantial growth and relative prosperity. The one aspect that casts a shadow over the antebellum South (and should have suggested increasing problems) was its attitude toward the resources of skills and knowledge. Conspicuously lower than the rest of the United States, the South's meager investment in education foreshadowed in the very long haul, its inability to diversify out of its dependence upon a few staple exports. The failure to invest in education, to raise the level of skills of both its whites and its former slave population continued long after the Civil War period, undoubtedly contributing to the miseries (compounded by the era of Reconstruction) that characterize the South for the rest of the nineteenth and into the twentieth century.

THE VIABILITY AND PROFITABILITY OF SLAVERY

A major issue of American history has been the viability of slavery. It has been contended that the slave system was unprofitable and that it would have toppled under its own weight without a Civil War, since the southerner would have been forced in the near future to replace the slave system with an alternative and more profitable form of economic activity. To some, the system seems to have been on its way to extinction.

In order to resolve this issue, it is important to distinguish clearly between two different parts of this controversy: (1) the viability of slavery and (2) the profitability of slavery in the production of cotton.

The viability of the institution of slavery is verified by the increasing desirability of owning slaves as reflected in rising prices for them. This rising price reflected an increasing demand for slaves (for whatever reasons) and therefore was an indication of the very opposite of a declining institution. The institution would become nonviable only if the price of slaves fell below the cost of rearing slaves. Instead, just the reverse was true: the gap between the cost of rearing slaves and the price of slaves was continuously widening. Since this divergence between slave prices and the cost of reproduction of slaves was so wide that it is not a matter of statistical controversy,[2] it is hard to understand any dispute over the viability of the institution.

The problem has been that the issue of viability has been mixed up with the profitability of slavery in cotton production. They are not the same thing. Southerners might be willing to hold slaves and bid up their price for reasons of prestige and not necessarily because of their direct economic value in cotton (or other plantation) production. A price of $1,800 for a prime hand might reflect his prestige value to a southern planter but not his value as a field hand.

The institution of slavery is a viable one under such conditions, even if the profitability of cotton has suffered thereby. One would become doubtful that such a state of affairs would last long,

---

[2] The difference between the net cost of rearing a slave and the price of a male slave (18 years old) has been calculated by Yasukichi Yasuba in "The Profitability and Viability of Plantation Slavery in the United States," *Economic Studies Quarterly*, XII, No. 1 (1961). This difference, adjusted for changes in the price level, was $334 in 1821-1825, rose to $668 in 1836-1840, fell to $585 in the depression years of 1841-1845, and then rose continually to $1,306 in 1856-1860.

however, since the same southerner depended on cotton production for his income and could not long afford to pay prestige prices for slaves if he were steadily losing money in raising cotton.[3]

In recent years, a number of studies have attempted to measure directly the profitability of slavery in the production of cotton. In a pioneering study, John Meyer and Alfred Conrad [4] have demonstrated that southern planters acted rationally in an economic sense in raising and selling slaves, in moving to better lands, and in adjusting cotton output to profitable opportunities. They also demonstrated that the rate of return on such activity was equal to alternative opportunities for using capital and that slavery in the immediate production of cotton was profitable. Conrad and Meyer's figures have been controversial, although the weight of evidence supports their position.[5] The conclusion we can draw, therefore, is that slavery was both a viable institution and profitable in cotton production for the South, however we may view it in retrospect in terms of its moral and ethical implications.

[3] If this were the case, the price of slaves would fall to a new equilibrium level that would bring into line the planter's income needs and his desire for conspicuous expenditure. If such a situation occurred, it would be a short-run disequilibrium situation but would in no way affect the viability of slavery.

[4] "The Economics of Slavery in the Ante Bellum South," *JPE*, LXVI, No. 2 (April 1958).

[5] See Richard Sutch, "The Profitability of Ante Bellum Slavery," *SEJ*, XXXI, No. 4 (April 1965).

chapter 8

GOVERNMENT
AND THE GROWTH
OF THE ECONOMY

We have already observed the crucial role played by the government in earlier days in the creation of a hospitable environment for economic activity. Development of a Constitution that provided for the honoring of contracts under a system of law and order was an essential step in protecting specific rights and obligations of private property. Equally important were certain early activities of the new government, particularly those initiated by Alexander Hamilton—development of a sound credit structure and other policies discussed in Chapter 4. It is hard to overestimate the importance of political stability and a society based on law for the development of a market economy. But beyond its functions in providing such a hospitable setting, how important was the active intervention of government in economic activity through public investment, tariffs, subsidies, land grants, and similar policies? [1]

In the past thirty years, a large number of studies have shown conclusively that government intervened significantly in the American economy in the nineteenth century. Early nineteenth century Massachusetts was a state in which government not only was involved in a variety of regulatory activity but provided a wide array

[1] This chapter is concerned with government subsidies and investment and does not explore other ways by which government may affect the performance of the economy, such as public land policy (Chap. 10) and monetary and fiscal policies (Chap. 13).

of subsidization of various kinds of economic activity. Even more striking was the case of Pennsylvania, where the government invested more than $100 million in public works, and where by 1844 there were public directors on the boards of more than 150 mixed (private and public) corporations. Other studies have shown that state governments in the South were major underwriters of railroad investment before the Civil War. Of $245 million invested in southern railroads in 1860, more than 55 per cent had been supplied through official public agencies. States invested more than $136 million in canals between 1815 and 1860. This was more than 73 per cent of canal investment. In Missouri, more than $23 million had been pledged to public improvement by 1860. State government investments declined in the post-Civil War period. Local aid was considerable in this period, and a large number of communities and counties spent substantial sums in encouraging or subsidizing transport development, particularly the development of railroads. The federal government also outdid the states by massive intervention in the form of 131 million acres in land grants to railroads for construction of transcontinental lines. This was in addition to approximately 48 million acres that were received by the railroads as state aid.

As a result of these studies, scholars have generally concluded that such governmental activity played a major part in accelerating the growth of the American economy. In a widely quoted review article, R. A. Lively summarizes the literature on the role of government as follows:

> Taken together, the works here reviewed form a consistent report of economic endeavor in an almost unfamiliar land. There, the elected public official replaced the individual enterpriser as the key figure in the release of capitalist energy; the public treasury, rather than private saving, became the major source of venture capital; and community purpose outweighed personal ambition in the selection of large goals for local economies. "Mixed" enterprise was the customary organization for important innovations, and government everywhere undertook the role put on it by the people, that of planner, promoter, investor, and regulator.[2]

---

[2] "The American System," *The Business History Review*, XXIX, No. 1 (March 1955), 81.

Caution, however, is clearly necessary at this point. It is one thing to point up the involvement of government at all levels in economic activity; it is still something else again to attribute to it a significant share of the growth of the American economy. As yet, there has been no systematic work that enables us to bridge this gap.[3] Unfortunately, all too often the present ideological attitudes of scholars toward government intervention have influenced their perspective on the past. What we need is an unbiased, systematic examination of the extent to which the activity of government at all levels did, or did not, actually promote economic growth. As of this date, no such analysis has been undertaken.

Again, the hypothetical alternative is essential here. We shall have to ask ourselves: What would have happened to the economy in the absence of government investment or promotion of a particular type of economic activity? During the nineteenth century, government's share of total reproducible wealth in the United States, like the realized income from government, was always a very small percentage of either total reproducible wealth or of national income. Crude estimates for the nineteenth century suggest that in each case it was not more than 5 per cent of the total.

Therefore, if government did in fact play a significant role in the economy, it must have been because its effects were larger than simply the quantitative data would assert. To state that such was the case, we must first have affirmative answers to the following theoretical issues: (1) Was the social rate of return upon investments in certain areas higher than the private rate of return? To put this in simpler language, were certain kinds of economic activity much more important and much more profitable to society as a whole (that is, in their social rate of return) than they would have been to private business firms (the private rate of return)? [4]

[3] A beginning in this direction was made by Harvey Segal in attempting to measure the benefits of canals in *Canals and American Economic Development* (New York: Columbia Univ., 1961), Chap. 5. A critical evaluation and a systematic attempt to estimate the benefits of the Ohio Canals are contained in Roger Ransom's "Canals and Development: A Discussion of the Issues," *AER*, LIV, No. 3 (May 1964).

[4] To take a simple illustration, a railroad that costs $100 million earns $10 million annually in net income. The private rate of return is 10 per cent. It also increases the income of farmers along its route, however (as a result of lower transport costs), by $10 million annually. The social rate of return is 20 per cent.

(2) Did the government deliberately and purposefully invest in activities in which there was a significant difference between the private and social rate of return? That is, such differences may well have existed, but it is quite another matter to assert that the government in fact was aware of these differences and was judicious in actually making the correct investments. (3) Was the magnitude of the social rate of return on government investment sufficiently large to make an appreciable contribution to the economy's rate of growth?

Lacking careful objective analysis, we can only resort to some impressionistic indications of particular aspects, which require further research. For example, take the first issue. Clearly, there were differences between private and social rates of return in a substantial number of economic activities. How important they were is hard to say. It is probably true that the capital market was imperfect in the early nineteenth century, and therefore it would have been hard for private individuals or for companies to amass sufficient capital to undertake certain economic activities that the state inaugurated. This was particularly true in the case of the canal era. It is widely held that the underwriting of canals by state governments made possible the attraction of foreign capital into such investment.[5] Certainly, there is evidence to suggest that this is in fact correct. It is also probable that the returns to society as a whole were greater in many transportation investments than returns would have been to a private investor, who would have been limited in the amount of tolls or rates he could have charged on a canal or a railroad. We may therefore cautiously conclude that in some significant areas there were important differences between the private and social rates of return in the economy in the nineteenth century.

Take the second point. Did the government, in fact, realize these differences—that is, was the government a wise investor? The investment of New York State in the Erie Canal immediately comes to mind. This was a brilliant venture that yielded handsomely to society. But in the same breath, we can mention the Pennsylvania

---

[5] It is important to realize that just because state government invested or made it possible to acquire capital from the London money market, that fact does not make government's contribution "indispensable." It simply means that otherwise the interest cost would have been higher or the project would have been delayed until it appeared more profitable to private investors.

TABLE 12. GOVERNMENT INVESTMENTS IN CANALS

State	Canal	Cost ($000)	
	I. *Probably successful:*		
N. Y.	Erie Canal	$7,143	
N. Y.	Champlain Canal	921	
N. Y.	Oswego Canal	2,512	
Ohio	Ohio Canal	4,245	
Pa.	Delaware Division Canal	1,543	
	Total successful canals		$16,364
	II. *Probably not successful:*		
Ohio	Miami and Erie Canal	5,920	
Ohio	Wahlhonding Canal	607	
Ohio	Hocking Canal	975	
Ohio	Wabash and Erie Canal	500	
N. Y.	Black River Canal	3,157	
N. Y.	Genesee Valley Canal	5,663	
N. Y.	Chenango Canal	2,316	
Pa.	Mainline Canal*	16,473	
Pa.	5 Penn. Lateral Canals†	15,033	
Ind.	Wabash Canal	6,325	
Ind.	Whitewater Canal	1,400	
Ill.	Illinois and Michigan	6,558	
Md.	Chesapeake and Ohio‡	11,071	
Va.	James and Kanawha§	10,436	
	Total unsuccessful canals		$86,434
	Total canal investment		102,798

* Mainline Canal cost includes railroad connections.

† The five canals were: the Susquehanna Division Canal, the French Creek Canal, Beaver Canal, the North Branch Division Canal, and the West Branch Division Canal.

‡ Private company whose stock was largely owned by Maryland, Virginia, and the United States government.

§ The $5.5 million of stock was purchased by Virginia, Richmond, and Lynchburg.

Source: Roger Ransom, "Canals and Development: A Discussion of the Issues," *AER*, LIV, No. 2 (May 1964), 375.

Main Line Canal, a rather spectacular and costly failure. When we assess the total investment in canals, the results are still inconclusive. Some, such as the Ohio canals in which the state government invested substantially, may or may not have been successful ventures and worthwhile for society. Others were clear failures and indeed went bankrupt very shortly. Roger Ransom cautiously summarizes the likely result of the major canal investments in the following table (Table 12). The same mixed pattern of results typifies many of the other states as well as the local underwriting of economic activity that took place in the nineteenth century. As a result, it is not possible at this point to assert one way or another what the outcome would look like if the necessary research were done.

Take the final issue that must be resolved. Even if necessary research to answer the first two questions had brought us to the conclusion that government investment was indeed a positive contribution, we would then have to know whether its magnitude was significant. For example, take 10 per cent as the government's percentage of gross capital formation in the nineteenth century, and assume that the social rate of return on *all* that investment was double that in the private sector. If the rate of growth of gross national product was 4.5 per cent per year, then the government's contribution would be 20 per cent of the contribution of capital to the growth rate.

Clearly, however, capital *alone* does not account for the total *extensive* and *intensive* growth of the economy—which is what the 4.5 per cent growth of GNP is measuring. That is, the 4.5 per cent figure measures increased output as a result *both* of the increase in inputs of productive factors and the increase in efficiency of productive factors. Population expansion of more than 80 million during the century and resultant increase in the labor force contribute an important part of the 4.5 per cent. Economies of scale that are not included would be another important contributor toward this growth rate. If, therefore, we say that capital contributed two-thirds of this rate of growth, then 20 per cent of 3 per cent is the government's contribution to the growth rate, or six-tenths of 1 per cent per year. Even this figure assumes that none of the resources devoted to government investment would have been replaced by private investment in the absence of such government intervention. If we assume more reasonably that one half of this investment would have been profitable for the private sector, then the contribution of government to the rate of growth would have been an increase in output of three-tenths of 1 per cent per year. This is certainly a significant figure, but it does not bear out statements that the role of local, state, and national government was indispensable. Since I have deliberately used figures that appear to be a substantial overstatement of the likely magnitudes, it would suggest that when we have done the necessary research, the *over-all* contribution of government investment in the nineteenth century will be a modest one.

If government's over-all contribution appears to have been limited, however, the rate of return upon specific activities may have been very high indeed.[6] Surprisingly, most of these activities appear to have received far less attention than those related to transport development. The most conspicuous is state and local government's contribution to education.[7] The development of the public school system appears to have been an important contribution to the growth of human capital in the United States. Similarly, with the passage of the Morrill Act in 1862, the land grant college made possible a wider spread of higher education than would have occurred in its absence. Unquestionably, private education would have experienced greater expansion in the absence of public education, but it would probably have resulted in a more unequal distribution of income than actually has prevailed. What was the social rate of return on education in nineteenth century America? Very little research has been done, but our present-day impression about the importance of human capital in economic development suggests that it was important and worthy of far more attention than it has received.

MEASUREMENTS OF THE CONTRIBUTION OF GOVERNMENT TO ECONOMIC GROWTH: RESEARCH IN AGRICULTURE

Is it possible to measure the contribution of government to the growth of output in a specific sector of the economy? The an-

---

[6] In fact, in subsequent pages of this chapter, I deliberately picked a case with extraordinary returns.

[7] In 1870 such investment was approximately 4 per cent of gross capital formation.

swer is clearly "yes." But instead of the impressionistic accounts that have characterized the studies in the past, we must use systematic economic analysis and empirical data to achieve any useful results. Take the case of government research in agriculture in the United States.

A recent study by John Kendrick [8] shows that productivity in agriculture increased very little between about 1900 and 1920, but thereafter rose very rapidly. Ever since 1887, with the passage of the Hatch Act, the federal government and numerous state agencies have expended substantial sums of money in research in agriculture.[9] What has been the contribution of this research to the observed productivity increase—that is, the social rate of return on this investment by the government? In the past fifteen years, economists have devoted a good deal of attention to measuring it.[10] In his *Economic Organization of Agriculture* [11] Professor Theodore Schultz presents systematic evidence to show a high rate of return on such investments by agencies of the United States Department of Agriculture as well as by state experiment stations. Instead of the over-all rate of return on research in agriculture (which Schultz estimates to be approximately 30 per cent), let us take one specific (and spectacularly successful) case—the social rate of return on the development of hybrid corn in the United States.[12]

Hybrid corn yields are 15 to 20 per cent higher than those of the earlier open-pollinated varieties. Using the hypothetical alternative, we may measure what the value of output would have been in the absence of hybrid corn, versus the value of output that actually existed as a result of its development. Against this value, we must ascertain the cost, meaning the total costs of the research expenditures in developing hybrid corn as well as any additional costs involved in using hybrid corn seed versus the open-pollinated

[8] *Productivity Trends in the United States* (Princeton, N.J.: Princeton Univ., 1961).

[9] An intriguing question is the failure of productivity to expand substantially until more than thirty years after the beginning of this research.

[10] I am very much indebted to Theodore W. Schultz for discussions and encouragement in writing this section of the study. The conclusions of course, are my own.

[11] (New York: McGraw-Hill, 1953), Chap. 7.

[12] The following section comes from Zvi Griliches, "Research Costs and Social Returns—Hybrid Corn and Related Innovations," *JPE*, LXVI, No. 5 (Oct. 1958).

Year	Total research expenditures (private and public)	Year	Total research expenditures (private and public)	Net social Returns*
1910	0.008	1933	0.584	0.3
1911	0.011	1934	0.564	1.1
1912	0.010	1935	0.593	2.9
1913	0.016	1936	0.661	8.3
1914	0.022	1937	0.664	21.2
1915	0.032	1938	0.721	39.9
1916	0.039	1939	0.846	60.3
1917	0.039	1940	1.090	81.7
1918	0.039	1941	1.100	105.3
1919	0.044	1942	1.070	124.3
1920	0.052	1943	1.390	140.4
1921	0.068	1944	1.590	158.7
1922	0.092	1945	1.600	172.6
1923	0.105	1946	1.820	184.7
1924	0.124	1947	1.660	194.3
1925	0.139	1948	1.660	203.7
1926	0.149	1949	1.840	209.8
1927	0.185	1950	2.060	209.0
1928	0.210	1951	2.110	218.7
1929	0.285	1952	2.180	226.7
1930	0.325	1953	2.030	232.1
1931	0.395	1954	2.270	234.2
1932	0.495	1955	2.790	239.1
		Annually after 1955	3.000	248.0

* Net of seed production cost but not net of research expenditures. Net social returns are zero before 1933.

Source: Zvi Griliches, "Research Costs and Social Returns: Hybrid Corn and Related Innovation," *JPE*, LXVI (Oct. 1958), 424. Reprinted by permission of The University of Chicago Press.

varieties.[13] Table 13 presents the results. As of 1955, for a research expenditure of $3 million, the net social returns were $248 million; or to put it more simply, the social rate of return on this investment, as of 1955, was at least 700 per cent.

The methods used here are similar to those of "benefit-cost analysis" which have been developed to measure the rate of return upon government investments, particularly in the field of water resources. It is clear that some kinds of returns are extremely difficult to quantify. Nevertheless, the development of this systematic method for measuring the rate of return upon government investment today points the way toward the kinds of research that are necessary to evaluate the contributions of government of yesterday.

[13] I am omitting from this discussion a large number of highly complex technical issues in economics, such as the problems of present worth, the appropriate interest rate, and the assumed supply and demand elasticities.

chapter 9

SHIPS,
RAILROADS,
AND ECONOMIC GROWTH

In American economic history, improvements in transportation in the nineteenth century have occupied a central place in explaining a substantial part of the economy's development. This is not surprising. The application of steam power to land and water transportation has appeared to most economic historians as the very epitome of the Industrial Revolution extending to transportation. It is to be expected, therefore, that the steamship on the one hand and the railroad on the other should have been deemed indispensable in the expansion of international trade and in promoting settlement and the economic development of a continent.

In addition to its revolutionary role in lowering transport costs, the railroad has also been credited with still further substantial effects upon economic development. The size of investment—that is, the amount of capital invested—in railroads in the United States in the nineteenth century made it the first billion-dollar industry by the time of the Civil War. Not only was it a large-scale industry; the railroad in the course of its building needed iron, steel, machinery, and timber; therefore, it was given credit for inducing expansion in still other industries. Finally, as a large-scale enterprise, the railroad required the development of sophisticated methods of large-scale business organization and has been looked upon as a pioneer in the development of corporate organization in the United States.

Impressions are no substitute for systematic analysis, however, which suggests a different interpretation of the role played by improving transportation in the nineteenth century economy. To put this role in perspective, let us carefully examine the changing costs of transportation, the investment induced by transportation enterprises, the organizational improvements effected by large-scale transportation media, and the relocation of economic activity as a result of changing transport costs.

Chart 18 provides us with an index of United States freight rates between 1814 and 1913 and can give us some notion of how ocean transportation costs fell in that century. The black line is an

CHART 18.   INDEX OF U.S. EXPORT FREIGHT RATES, 1814-1913

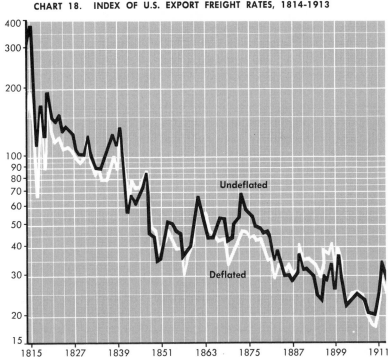

Source: Douglass C. North, "The Role of Transportation in the Economic Development of North America," paper presented to The International Congress of the Historical Sciences (Vienna, August 1965) and published in *Les grandes voies maritimes dans le monde xvᵉ-xixᵉ siècles* (Paris, 1965).

index of freight rates themselves over this period, and the white line is one in which the freight rate index is divided by a price index for the period, so that we can attempt to see how the freight rates fell—adjusted to changes in the general price level. The chart shows that the most striking fall of ocean freight rates occurred between 1815 and 1850, followed by a period in which freight rates fell very little. Then they fell somewhat more modestly in the years between 1873 and 1908.

Although the steamship substituted for the sailing ship in passenger travel as early as 1850, it did not substitute for the sailing ship in the carriage of bulk goods in ocean transportation until much later. Indeed, as late as 1880 most of the goods carried in ocean transportation were going by sail, and the changeover from sail to steam did not occur in most of the long-haul routes in the world until the very end of the nineteenth century, when the triple-expansion engine made it possible for steam to compete effectively with sail. Some routes, such as the long haul of grain from the Pacific Northwest to Liverpool, 14,000 miles around Cape Horn, were still dominated by sailing ships right up until World War I. In short, it took the steamship approximately eighty years from its inception at the beginning of the nineteenth century to replace the sailing ship in the carriage of most bulk commodities. Yet, the striking feature of the chart is that the fall in transportation rates is most rapid in a period when sail dominated ocean shipping; therefore, the improvements in efficiency must be attributed primarily to the sailing ship. Even after 1870, improvement in sailing-ship efficiency continued to enable the sailing vessel to compete with the steamship right up until the end of the century. Clearly, it was the sailing ship and not the steamship that was responsible in good part for the dramatic fall in ocean transportation costs in the nineteenth century.

Chart 19 summarizes the fall in inland freight rates between 1784 and 1900. Since changes in the price level are not taken out of this chart, some of the movement reflects changes in general prices rather than real falls in transportation costs themselves. The pattern of rate changes is so great, however, that such a bias does not really alter the picture very much. Here, one can see that the major decline in inland transportation rates is a result of the contrast between wagon and water rates. Note that the upstream and downstream

CHART 19.   GENERAL PATTERN OF INLAND FREIGHT RATES, 1784-1900
(Cents per ton-mile)

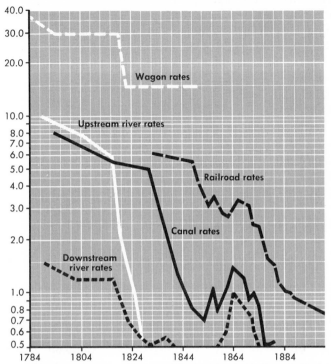

Source: Douglass C. North, ''The Role of Transportation in the Economic Development of North America.''

river rates and canal rates are consistently lower throughout than railroad rates. The dramatic effect of technological change in inland transportation is not the advent of the railroad (which is the one that we customarily think of), but rather the development of the steamship on inland waters. The consequent fall in rates of upstream river transportation after 1816 directly reflects the use of steamboats on the Mississippi River and its tributaries. Here is clearly a case of technological development playing a significant part in lowering transportation costs.

Railroad rates fell dramatically throughout the century, but

CHART 20.   EXPANSION OF RAILROAD MILEAGE, 1830-1890
(In miles of road operated)

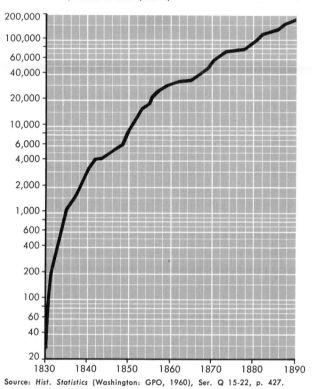

Source: *Hist. Statistics* (Washington: GPO, 1960), Ser. Q 15-22, p. 427.

as noted above, they remained higher than water rates. The railroad's domination of inland transportation during the last half of the nineteenth century, therefore must have been due to reasons other than the direct one of simply offering lower ton-mile rates. This is the subject to be examined at the end of this chapter.

The expansion of the railroad into every corner of the United States in the nineteenth century was certainly a dramatic event, graphically indicated by Chart 20. The expansion of railroad mileage gives a clue to the way in which the railroad came to be the dominant medium of internal transportation, and the investment necessary to build this immense system is recorded in Table 14. But

TABLE 14. PROPERTY INVESTMENT IN RAILROADS, 1850-1890
(In thousands of dollars)

Year	Total
1850	$ 318,126
1851	————
1855	763,678
1860	1,149,481
1861	————
1863	————
1867	1,172,881
1868	1,869,529
1869	2,041,226
1870	2,476,893
1871	2,664,628
1872	3,159,423
1873	3,784,543
1874	4,221,764
1875	4,658,209
1876	4,468,592
1877	4,806,202
1878	4,772,297
1879	4,872,018
1880	5,402,038
1881	6,278,565
1882	7,016,750
1883	7,477,866
1884	7,676,399
1885	7,842,533
1886	8,163,149
1887	8,673,187
1888	9,369,399
1889	9,680,942
1890	10,122,636

Source: *Hist. Statistics*, Ser. Q33-42, p. 428.

induced investment is not, itself, a gain to the economy (as we saw in Chapter 6), since the improved productivity has already been passed on in the form of lower rates in the transportation medium itself. Therefore, investments in other kinds of enterprises—iron, steel, timber, machinery, and so forth—are an expansion for the economy only to the extent that they make possible lower costs in that industry, costs that would not have been reduced without the demand on the part of the railroad. Since this subject has already been examined, no further discussion will be made here.

A further point does need examination: the role of the railroad in the development of sophisticated large-scale organization. The railroad clearly was the first large-scale enterprise in America, the kind of enterprise that required a corporate form of organization and the solving of complex problems of efficient development. It is difficult to assess the importance of the railroad's role in this process of improved organization. One is tempted to believe that it was a dependent variable, in the sense that—given the gradual development of large-scale enterprise—a learning process would inevitably have taken place, whatever the industry was. Since manufacturing was also developing large-scale organization by the end of the nineteenth century, such improvement of efficiency might very well have happened without any more growing pains, as a result of expansion in the size of the manufacturing firm.

The development and financing of the railroad in the nineteenth century was not an unmitigated gain, even if we do acknowledge that it paved the way to improvements in organization in general. Some aspects of railroad financing and organization in the United States in the nineteenth century were clearly a detriment. The financial manipulations of railroad financiers in the decades from the 1870's to 1900 are familiar history—manipulations that led to substantial watering of the stock, that is, to expansion in the amount of nominal capital without really increasing the tangible earning power of the railroad. The result was a series of titanic battles between railroad financiers, in which frequently bondholders —and they were often British bondholders—suffered at the expense of these manipulators. The era of Drew, Fisk, and Gould in the Erie Railroad is a famous episode but not an isolated one. It was not until the very end of the century that wild railroad financing schemes came to an end. Clearly, these had involved some costs to improving organization, in the sense that they had made risks higher. American and English investors were more reluctant to invest in railroads than they would have been had the management been more responsible. Railroad finance, therefore, was a detriment to improvement of economic organization and to improvements in the capital market. The actual costs have never been ascertained; but they doubtless were of some significance and afford a counterweight to whatever importance attaches to the railroad as an agent in improving our knowledge about large-scale business organization.

Falling costs of transportation, particularly ocean transportation, show little evidence of relocating major forms of economic activity in the United States. Perhaps their greater impact was on other countries—for example, the dramatic fall in the inland and

TABLE 15. EMPLOYMENT IN MANUFACTURING BY REGION AS A PER CENT OF U.S.

	1859	1869	1879	1889	1899	1904	1909	1914
New England	29.88	26.76	24.31	20.57	18.91	17.87	17.30	16.83
Mid. Atlantic	41.66	39.52	42.04	38.69	37.54	36.99	35.82	35.89
Great Lakes	12.09	18.36	19.19	22.29	22.65	22.29	22.73	23.73
Southeast	9.80	8.48	7.57	8.90	11.55	12.87	13.61	13.05
Plains	2.30	4.79	4.46	6.01	5.41	5.37	5.32	5.10
Southwest	0.34	0.37	0.44	0.67	0.79	0.97	1.26	1.30
Mountain	0.03	0.17	0.31	0.49	0.71	0.69	0.82	0.82
Far West	3.90[a]	1.54	1.70	2.37	2.43	2.93	3.14	3.26

[a] Including gold mining.

Source: Figures for 1859 are from U.S. Census Office, *The Eighth Census: Manufactures of the United States in 1860* (Washington: GPO, 1865). These are the raw "number of hands employed" figures and are not strictly comparable with subsequent years.

From 1869 to 1909 inclusive, figures are from Richard A. Easterlin, "Estimates of Manufacturing Activity," *Population Redistribution and Economic Growth, United States, 1870-1950,* (Philadelphia: The American Philosophical Society, 1957), I, 684. These figures have been adjusted from original census data in several ways and are rounded to the nearest hundreds.

Figures for 1914 are based on the "average wage earners" category of U.S. Census Office, *Abstract of the Census of Manufactures, 1914* (Washington: GPO, 1917). In order to make them roughly comparable to the 1869-1909 data, percentage changes from 1909 to 1914 in the census figures were calculated, and these were applied to the 1909 figures from the above source. This assumes that structural changes in employment were not great between 1909 and 1914.

ocean transportation costs in carrying grain and other foodstuffs to Europe hastened the relative decline of European agricultural production. The development of the North Pacific grain trade from Seattle and Portland to Liverpool was a case in point. Here, a major new wheat-producing area was brought into the world market by two factors: a fall of inland transportation costs of getting wheat from the inland empire to Seattle and Portland, combined with savings effected by a more efficient ocean transportation route around Cape Horn. But this is perhaps the most dramatic case in which transportation costs by sea had an effect upon the development of a new economic activity.

To what extent was economic activity internally relocated by the railroad? Table 15 shows the distribution of manufacturing by employment among the various regions from 1859 to 1914. It is apparent that New England declined substantially and the Middle Atlantic states slightly, during this period, while other areas increased their manufacturing share. The Southeast declined until 1879 and then grew substantially. The Far West grew at a later period, and the Plains states grew slightly. How much of this changing pattern of economic activity was due to the railroads? Some part of it surely was. The shift of textiles out of New England into the South probably was accounted for, at least in part, by the growth of railroad transportation in the South in later years. Some other industries were resource oriented, and the availability of the railroad made it possible for plants to be nearer to the natural resources. The usefulness of timberlands and other natural resources was certainly increased by the development of the railroad. On the other hand, it was the modification, rather than initiation, of industrial activities for which the railroad could take credit in certain areas, particularly in the Middle Atlantic and Great Lakes states. There the transportation needs were already met by water, and the railroad led, at most, to rather minor relocations of industrial activity.

It is clear that the acceleration of the settlement and agricultural output of the western two-thirds of the United States was strikingly influenced by the advent of the railroad. Maps 1 and 2 present evidence of the railroad's influence upon settlement and agricultural output. Map 1 shows population density and transportation facilities in Illinois in 1850. Note that density was greatest in the peripheral counties where cheap water transportation was available (as well as along navigable waterways). In the next ten years, approximately 2,700 miles of railroad opened up the whole interior of the state, and the results are shown in Map 2. The agricultural output showed correspondingly striking gains.[1] The shift of the wheat industry westward into the Great Plains and the opening of new agricultural areas where no feasible water transportation was available reflected the impact of railroad transportation upon relocation of agriculture. Even here, however, its significance can be overstated. Robert Fogel has estimated (see following) that while less than half the land mass of the United States in 1890 was within forty miles of a navigable waterway, more than three quarters of the agricultural land was within such limits, the limits of feasible commercial agriculture. The great bulk of the land outside these limits was between the 100 meridian and the Sierra Nevada mountains; and as of 1890, it produced only 2 per cent of the country's agricultural products.

THE INDISPENSABILITY OF THE RAILROAD
FOR AMERICAN ECONOMIC GROWTH

Two recent excellent studies of the railroad in the nineteenth century enable us to determine more precisely its contribution to the economic growth of the United States [2] and to estimate what the national income might have been without railroads. With respect to the United States in 1890, Robert Fogel divides his study into two major parts: (1) the loss in income that would have resulted in the United States had there been no interregional transportation by railroad, and (2) the loss in income that would have resulted had there been no intraregional railroads. Let us take each in turn.

---

[1] See Douglass C. North, *The Economic Growth of the United States, 1790-1860* (Englewood Cliffs, N.J.: Prentice-Hall, 1961), pp. 146-53. Additional discussion of this subject is provided in a forthcoming study by Albert Fishlow, *The Economic Contribution of American Railroads before the Civil War.*

[2] Robert W. Fogel, *Railroads in American Economic Growth* (Baltimore: Johns Hopkins, 1964), and Albert Fishlow, *Economic Contribution of American Railroads* (forthcoming study).

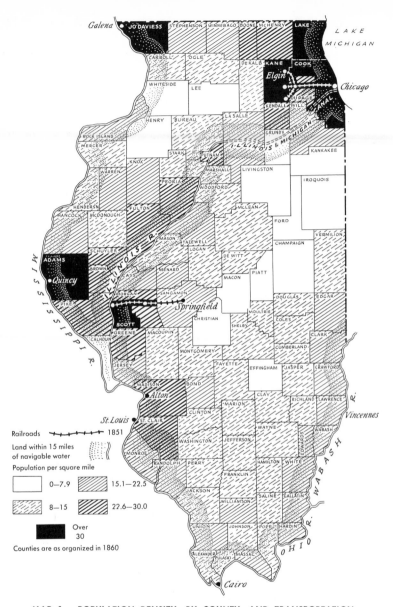

MAP 1. POPULATION DENSITY, BY COUNTY, AND TRANSPORTATION FACILITIES, ILLINOIS, 1850

Source: Douglass C. North, *The Economic Growth of the United States, 1790-1860* (Englewood Cliffs, N.J.: Prentice-Hall, 1961), p. 147.

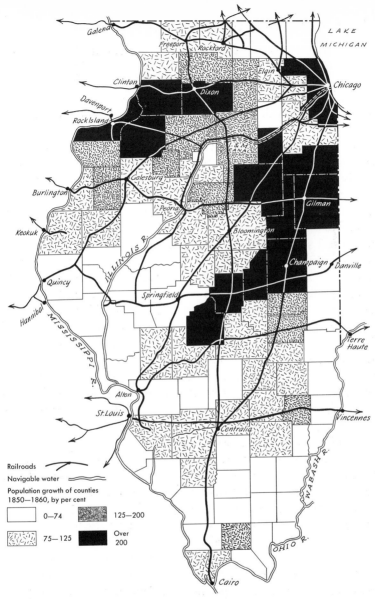

**MAP 2. POPULATION DENSITY, BY COUNTY, AND TRANSPORTATION
FACILITIES, ILLINOIS, 1861 (APRIL 1)**

Source: Douglass C. North, *The Economic Growth of the United States, 1790-1860*, p. 149.

Fogel measures the actual costs of movement of agricultural goods from the major collection centers in the internal United States to the major consuming points by railroad, and then measures what the costs would have been had they moved by the next best alternative, which would have meant some wagon haul but primarily movement by water. It must be remembered that the eastern half of the United States was well endowed with water transportation routes on the complex of canals, the Great Lakes, and the Mississippi River system. Since we have already noted that water rates were lower than rail rates, it is not surprising that the first approximation shows that movement by water would have been actually cheaper than by rail. Against this negative figure, however, the railroad had some significant advantages that turned it into a positive figure. The cargo losses would have been higher by water. There would have been substantially higher transshipment costs. Moreover, because water routes are frozen over a part of the year, much higher storage or inventory of goods would have been required, since the routes would have been unusable for that period (but this simply is the additional cost of the necessary inventory). Additional wagon hauls to get the goods to water would have also been higher. The result is—as indeed it must be, since the railroad does in fact replace water—that the railroad provided a positive gain in interregional trade. But the size of the gain is quite surprising. It comes by Fogel's estimation to approximately $73 million, which is 6/10 of 1 per cent of gross national product in 1890.

The problems of estimating the losses that would have resulted had there been no railroad in intraregional trade are more complex and involve more technical analysis. The estimate that Fogel arrives at varies between $248 million and $337 million, or between 2.1 per cent and 2.8 per cent of gross national product. Fogel points out that these are clearly too high, since he has not allowed for any readjustment of economic activity or of extension of waterways, which would have resulted had there been no railroad. Fogel's figures so far have been for agricultural commodities only. Using the same principle and extending it to all commodities, the total social saving attributable to the railroad comes to approximately 4.7 per cent of gross national product, again not allowing for any adaptation of other transport media in the absence of the railroad.[3]

Fogel's analysis makes clear that the contribution of the railroad was not anything like the impressionistic notions that we have derived from earlier economic history. Yet, at this point it should be noted *very carefully* that even if the figure of 5 per cent of gross national product is somewhat less than two years' growth in the economy—that is, without the railroad the economy would have had the gross national product of 1888 rather than 1890—we know of few, if any, other innovations that have had such a great effect. A social saving of 5 per cent is a very substantial saving. It is startlingly low only when put in the context of our traditional magnified impressions. One of the most important lessons to be learned from this study is that probably no single industry accounts for any major share in the development of an economy. Rather, it is a complex development in which improvements in efficiency stem from the totality of economic activity rather than immense jumps in productivity coming from a few industries.

[3] In Albert Fishlow's forthcoming study he suggests that a somewhat higher social saving is attributable to railroads. In fact, he has a 5 per cent figure for 1860. I have not had the opportunity of seeing all of Fishlow's manuscript, but what I have seen suggests that his figure is a generous upper-limit estimate. The difference between Fogel and Fishlow, however, is not very great when compared to the widely-held views of the railroad's indispensability.

chapter 10

LAND POLICY AND
THE WESTWARD MOVEMENT,
1785-1890

Perhaps the most dramatic episode in American economic history is the settling and populating of our share of this continent. A vast area was settled in America between 1776 and the 1890's, when the superintendent of the U.S. Census reported that the frontier had disappeared in America. At the time of the Declaration of Independence, only the eastern seaboard was settled, although some pioneers had crossed the mountains and established themselves in the area on the other side of the Appalachian Mountains, in the Ohio Valley. Farther west, the country was for the most part unknown to white men.

Over these years the United States acquired lands in big chunks: the Louisiana Purchase, embracing all of the area acquired from the French in 1803; Florida in 1819; and Texas, California, and the territory of Oregon in the 1840's. By 1853, with the Gadsden Purchase of a strip on the Mexican border, the contiguous territorial boundaries of the continental Unted States had been filled out.

Settling and populating these areas was a much longer, dramatic story that begins with the expedition of Lewis and Clark. These two, with their party, followed the Missouri River system to its headwaters, crossed the Rocky Mountains, traveled down the Columbia, and wintered at its mouth. When they returned, they

122

told a story of an extraordinary land, full of promise, full of prospects—a land that was to dominate much of our history for the rest of the century, as venturesome Americans successively looked over the new frontier and settled it. Fur traders came hard on the heels of Lewis and Clark. In fact, some members of their expedition turned right around and went back up river to search for beaver pelts. Following the fur trader came the farmer and the miner, and settlements developed as the frontier receded westward. The center of population continued to move west as this immense expanse of territory was settled and developed in the nineteenth century.

Geographical expansion has been an exciting story and one that has preoccupied our attention. It has also presented extraordinary economic problems beginning with the Constitution itself, when the federal government was permitted to gain title to lands within the states. An important decision early in the history of this nation was that these lands would not be retained by the government, but would be disposed of for private ownership.

The point decided, the government had a number of different and sometimes contradictory objectives that could be advanced by the sale of public lands. Its prime objective was to aid and abet the

TABLE 16. MAJOR ACTS AFFECTING LAND DISTRIBUTION, 1785-1832

Act	Minimum unit in acres	Minimum auction price per acre	Terms of sale
1785	640	$1.00	Cash, ½ by township; ½ by sections
1796	640	2.00	½ cash, ½ credit for 1 yr.
1800	320	2.00	¼ cash; ¼ in 2 yrs.; ¼ in 3 yrs.; ¼ in 4 yrs.
1804	160	2.00	Same as in 1800
1820	80	1.25	Cash
1832	40	1.25	Cash

Source: Philip H. Overmeyer, "Westward Expansion Before the Homestead Act," in *Growth of the American Economy* (2nd ed.), ed. Harold F. Williamson (Englewood Cliffs, N.J.: Prentice-Hall, 1951), p. 104.

settlement of the United States and to create conditions that would favor economic development. But it also wanted to raise revenue; and public land sales proved to be a major, although very irregular source of revenue for a long period in our history.

There was an endless variety of possible methods for making these lands available to the public, and their disposal has become one of the most controversial subjects in American history. A look at Table 16 shows how public land sales changed between 1785 and 1832 under the impact of congressional legislation.

The first act, in 1785, not only set minimum standards for sales, in terms of unit size and price, but also laid out the whole "township" system of division that has characterized surveying ever since. Less durable were the minimum standards. These shifted drastically, as the table indicates, dropping from 640 acres in 1785 to 40 acres in 1832. The minimum price per acre, meantime, started at $1.00, went to $2.00 until 1804, and then dropped to $1.25 between 1820 and 1832. The terms, cash or credit, varied. The general system of distribution was to put the lands up for auction. If no one bid above the set minimum, that land remained unsold.

Ever since the Revolution, the government had given away substantial tracts. Veterans of wars received military bounty warrants entitling them to land; and as large numbers of these warrants accumulated from earlier wars, they came to be traded actively, so that they were bought and sold like any other equity. As noted in previous chapters, both the federal government and the state gave public lands to the railroads, to encourage the building of transcontinental systems. A total of 180 million acres went toward this objective, with the Northern Pacific receiving the lion's share, but other lines also benefiting greatly.

In 1841, the Pre-emption Act was put into effect to protect squatters, those eager settlers who had gone out ahead of the surveyers and, holding no title to their land, found themselves faced with eviction, sometimes by government troops. The new act gave squatters first rights to purchase their land if they had settled on it before survey and before its disposal at public auction. In 1854 a Graduation Act was passed. Lands that had not sold at the government minimum were now permitted to be sold at lower prices. Then came the great landmark enactment that has frequently been thought of as dividing the history of America's public lands—the Homestead Act. This act, in 1862, stipulated that a bonafide settler could receive title to 160 acres free and clear (or 320 acres if he were married) provided that he lived on the land and improved it for a certain period and in certain terms. As time went on, it became clear that additional acts were needed, particularly in areas where mining and lumbering were involved, and this led to the Timber Culture Act in 1873, the Desert Act of 1877, and the Timber Cutting Act and Timber and Stone Act of 1878.[1]

This long history of legislation delineating the government's position on public land sales has been the target of endless invective. In general, historians have been extremely critical of the whole system, feeling that it rewarded greed and speculation. There is no doubt that speculation in public lands was a favorite occupation of Americans in the nineteenth century. Not only big speculators went out, bought vast tracts of land ahead of settlement, and attempted to sell them as settlers moved west, but smaller holders speculated, too. Many a farmer bought more land than he could possibly cultivate, with the idea of holding it for a rise in value. As a result, speculation is blamed for discouraging actual farming and encouraging the view of land as a speculative commodity. It is also alleged that the westward movement was impaired by the system of land disposal that left large tracts of land unsettled for a long time, either because the minimum price was too high or because speculators were holding the land off the market for a higher price. Critics have also contended that the economic growth of the country was hampered by this disposition of land, partly because of the inhibition of settlement that resulted from holding land off the market and partly from the fact that the kinds of land acts were not best suited to the particular needs of the times—that is, in the early period of rich lands, large tracts were specified as a minimum; but in the later period, when nonarable pasture characterized the land, the maximum size under the Homestead Act was far too small for an efficient farm unit.

Also, historians have felt that the national distribution of wealth was adversely affected by the way that lands were given

[1] These acts were designed to encourage tree growing, to aid in settlement and irrigation of desert areas, and to dispose of timber lands.

away: monopolists, speculators, and the rich were favored at the expense of the hardworking farmer and the poor settler. It is a generally held view that one aim in disposal of public lands should have been to assure that the wage earner and the poor in the East had a safety valve, a way to escape the city and poverty. Before re-examining these criticisms in more detail, it will be helpful to take an economist's-eye view of the whole process of the westward movement and how it was instigated. In part, it was simply people moving to escape the urban life, the life of settlements; venturesome people wanted to go out into the wilds; some (like the Mormons) wanted to escape what they felt was religious persecution. But escape was only a part of the motive force in westward movement. The typical pattern of settlement was guided by economic motives— people went West because they felt that they could better themselves economically, in light of America's burgeoning demand for agricultural goods, mining output, and lumber. As population grew and the demand for products increased, particularly for crops to feed the industralized and urbanized East, the West offered improving opportunity to supply this need.

We are familiar with the way in which a market economy, through price changes, automatically meets such needs. In this case, the demand was not only from the expanding East, but from foreigners as well. Before the Civil War, cotton was the leading export. Wheat had come into prominence as an export at the time of the Irish Famine in the 1840's and gained great momentum after the war. Ample lands were available for agricultural expansion; the limiting factor was transportation, but we have already traced the way this problem was solved. Canals and waterways in the eastern half of the United States provided an effective medium for carrying regional goods to market; then the railroad entered the plains and the prairies, providing transportation where no effective waterway existed. To balance the scales for westward settlement, then, it is evident that on the demand side people were influenced by the growing need for farm goods, lumber, and mining goods; on the supply side, transportation was opening up new areas to make all this production possible. These developments should be reflected in the action of prices, and that is exactly the way they do show up. Surges of movement into new lands occurred in 1816-1818, the

1830's, the 1850's, the late 1860's, and in the 1880's; and each of these surges was induced by a rapidly expanding demand for goods and by rising prices of agricultural goods.[2] It is well to keep this in mind, because such market influences do not appear as decisive in many descriptions of westward settlement. The view that the West not only dominated our history but that it was a refuge in bad times for the poor and unemployed is simply untenable. The unemployed and the poor in general did not have the means to go West and start farming. Moreover, most people moved West in good times. They moved West in periods of rising prices, of expanding demand, when the prospects for making money from this new land looked brightest; and this aspect characterized the whole pattern of settlement.

If the foregoing summary of historians' criticisms suggests that they have reached consensus upon the inadequacies of the country's public land policy, such is not the case. In fact, as the following quotations from leading authorities indicate, the subject is in a state of substantial confusion.

> Homeseekers in the West, being unwilling to go far afield from means of transportation or to settle upon the inferior lands remaining open to homestead, and lacking capital with which to purchase farms and to provide equipment for them, were frequently forced to become tenants on the lands of speculators. Thus farm tenancy developed in the frontier stage at least a generation before it would have appeared had the homestead system worked properly.[3]

> We can see now that the price of land was not the critical determinant in the success of the authentic farm maker. An eighty-acre farm at $1.25 an acre would cost him $100. This was only a small fraction of his total farm-making costs. If he lacked the skills and the capital necessary to develop a farm, free land wouldn't help him.[4]

[2] A fall in transport costs or *any improvement* in the prospective income of the farmer would produce these results.

[3] Paul Wallace Gates, "The Homestead Law in an Incongruous Land System," *AHR*, XLI, No. 4 (July 1936), 670.

[4] Thomas LeDuc, "History and Appraisal of U.S. Land Policy to 1862," *Land Use Policy and Problems in the United States*, ed. Howard W. Ottoson (Lincoln: U. of Nebraska, 1963), p. 26.

In fact, however, the government steadily offered more land than the market could absorb at the minimum price and the auction system soon became a joke. So much first-class land was offered that bids never rose much above the minimum, speculative buying was encouraged, a lot of land remained unsold, and so far as any settlement followed sale, it was scattered among tracts of idle land in public or in speculative hands.[5]

This continued monopolization of the best lands and the resulting growth of farm tenancy led reformers and others who feared the establishment of a landed aristocracy similar to that existing in many European countries to advocate the ending of the cash sales system entirely.[6]

Speculator ownership and tenancy did not always result in the best use of the land. It has already been seen that speculator ownership forced widespread dispersion of population and placed heavy tax burdens upon farmers, whose improved lands could be more heavily assessed than the speculators' unimproved land. Furthermore, speculators were slow to pay taxes. They resisted increased levies, secured injunctions against expenditures for buildings and roads, and sometimes simply refused to pay taxes. Heavy interest penalties and tax titles did not trouble them particularly, since they knew they could later make a compromise settlement with the hard-pressed county boards, or could have the tax titles set aside by the courts.[7]

Moneylenders, land speculators, and gamblers in town lots now found themselves loaded with financial burdens which they could not carry. Their land was unsalable, yet their taxes continued to mount, as did also the interest on the money they had borrowed. Having invested everything in property not easily liquidated, they now were forced to surrender much of their land to the banks when these institutions began to call in their loans. The abstracts of conveyances for the years following the Panic of 1837 show a tremendous volume of mortgage foreclosures of large estates. . . .

[5] *Ibid.,* p. 5.

[6] Gates, *AHR,* XLI, 670.

[7] Paul Wallace Gates, "The Role of the Land Speculator in Western Development," *Pennsylvania Magazine of History and Biography,* LXVI, No. 3 (July 1942); reprinted in *The Public Lands,* ed. Vernon Carstensen, (Madison: U. of Wisconsin, 1963), p. 361.

During the bleak years of the early forties, the equity of absentees was gradually eaten up by tax titles, agents' costs, interest, and depredations. Ultimately the burden became too great, and many sold their holdings for less than the original cost, disregarding interest, fees, and taxes.[8]

When newly surveyed lands were first announced for sale, the squatters had to arrange for the purchase of their lands—made valuable by their improvements—before the opening of the auction, or run the risk of losing them to speculators.[9]

The theoretical defense of pre-emption was that the squatters were public beneficiaries engaged in actual development of the West. Exposing to public auction the tracts they had improved would permit others to confiscate the fixed improvements by purchasing the fee in the land. The defect in this theory is that the alleged improvements were generally negligible in value if not altogether invisible.[10]

Loan sharks were present at every public land auction, and their agents were stationed in every land-office town, prepared to buy claims for squatters. The 10 or 12 per cent allowed by the usury laws did not satisfy these moneylenders, who found it possible to evade such restrictions. They would buy claims on which squatters had their improvements, according to previous agreements, and would then resell the land to them for an advance of $30 above cost on a quarter section. The squatter would agree to pay at the end of one or two years the maximum interest allowed by law. If the legal interest was 12 per cent and the debt was paid in one year, the lender would net 28 per cent upon his investment. The loan agents always denied that they were violating the usury laws, but they were exceedingly loath to have cases involving their transactions taken into the courts. Thousands of desperate squatters throughout the West snatched at the aid offered by the moneylenders who personally or through land agents invested many millions of dollars in this lucrative business.[11]

Many western settlers had larceny in their hearts when it came to dealing with the government, and it did not stretch their con-

[8] *Ibid.*, pp. 358-59.
[9] *Ibid.*, p. 356.
[10] LeDuc, *op. cit.*, p. 12.
[11] Gates, in *The Public Lands*, p. 357.

sciences unduly to take advantage of the insurance companies or other absentee sources of capital. As one insurance adjuster later said, "it became really too easy for settlers to cash in on their western venture and 'go back to their wives' folks.' They borrowed more than the land was worth and fled." An agent for a Kansas bank said of the borrowers in western Kansas: "As soon as their loans are completed they abandon the land, if they can sell it to someone for a nominal sum above the mortgage they do so." [12]

The trouble with the Homestead Act in operation, as with the Pre-emption Act, was that Congress merely adopted the law and then did absolutely nothing in the way of helping the needy persons out to the land or extending them credit and guidance in the first heartbreaking years of occupancy. Perhaps these functions were outside the scope of federal authority, at least as then conceived, but without them the Homestead Act could benefit only monopolists or persons of fairly ample means.[13]

How significant was the Homestead Law in enabling settlers to acquire land and to establish themselves on going farms? It is clear that it was most successful in the period from 1863 to 1880 when the greater proportion of homesteads were being established in the states bordering on the Mississippi River. It was successful also in parts of Kansas and Nebraska well east of the 98th meridian where there was abundance of rain, and where commutations, relinquishments, and abandonments were fewer than they were to be in other areas later. In these eighteen years, homesteaders filed on 469,000 tracts and by 1885 had made their final entries and were in process of getting title on 55 per cent. Doubtless some would complete their residence requirements in later years.[14]

The land-use pattern of the twenty-nine public land states of the South, the Middle West, and the Far West is the result of a long process of development and adaptation in which such factors as

[12] Paul Wallace Gates, "The Homestead Act: Free Land Policy in Operation, 1862-1935," *Land Use Policy and Problems in the United States, op. cit.,* p. 36.
[13] Fred A. Shannon, "The Homestead Act and the Labor Surplus," *AHR,* XLI, No. 4 (July 1936), 644.
[14] Gates, in *Land Use Policy,* p. 41.

speculation, absentee ownership, credit usury, farm mechanization, transportation, and government controls have played important roles. Only recently has the United States come to realize the monstrous errors it permitted to develop in this land-use pattern. Likewise, only recently has it become apparent that this pattern is the product in part of mistaken land policies which were once thought to be establishing a democratic system of landownership.[15]

These quotations do more than simply show the contradictory interpretive positions that riddle the literature on the subject. They point up the inability of the historian to come to grips with the problems without the systematic use of theory to examine the issues and the testing of resultant hypotheses by careful empirical research. I do not mean to suggest that each and every quotation is not founded upon some detailed story of the vast panorama of settlement of the public domains. It is. And this very fact reflects the immensely rich and varigated story of this westward movement. But from these particular stories, the historian has generalized the consequences of the entire public land policies. It would be possible to accumulate an endless number of such stories, but they do not add up to an over-all appraisal of the policies. If we are to assert that the policies adversely affected economic growth, then we must assess the policies in terms of the determinants of economic growth; or if we are to assess them in terms of their effects upon welfare or equity, we must do so in terms of a careful examination of the consequences of the policies on the distribution of income.

EFFECT OF PUBLIC LAND POLICIES ON GROWTH AND WELFARE IN THE NINETEENTH CENTURY

Since preliminary spadework has not been done, conclusions must be limited; but at least we can precisely define the issues, suggest some hypotheses that must be tested, and explore the existing systematic evidence that might bear upon these hypotheses.

Examination of public land policies, to determine their effect on growth and welfare in the nineteenth century is complicated

[15] Gates, in *The Public Lands*, p. 349.

by (1) the number and variety of laws related to public land policies; (2) the wide variety of types of land and resources that were exploited in the course of the westward movement; (3) inadequate, poor administration of public land policies; and (4) graft and corruption that was characteristic of all levels and all kinds of people involved in the settlement of the public domain.

Continuous repetition of the words "speculator" and "land monopolization" throughout the literature requires precise examination of these terms before we can go further. Just what does constitute speculation? When anyone buys an asset with a resale value, he is indulging in speculation. Buying that asset, he foregoes buying other assets, all offering prospective income streams that he takes into account. He is guessing about the future value of that asset. In contemplating the purchase of a fixed-yield bond, for example, he speculates not only that he will get the specified return, but whether the general level of prices will rise or fall, so that actually his return will be of lesser or greater value than was indicated. Speculation is endemic to any system of private ownership of assets. It is therefore hard to imagine any way that one could dispose of public lands without speculation. Moreover, the speculator performs the important function of bearing risks in a market economy and of improving knowledge about the available alternative opportunities, thereby making the market work more perfectly.

The term "land monopolist" is simply a misuse of "monopolist." There is no meaningful sense in which a monopoly of land existed at any time in the nineteenth century. In fact, availability is the one clearly evident characteristic of the opening up of the public domain. There were immense amounts of land continuously available from a large number of different sources. People who wanted land of any quality could always get it from a host of sellers in addition to the government. Merely to record that large blocks of land were at times bought by individuals is in no sense an indication of land monopoly, unless the buyers actually acquired such an appreciable percentage of all available land that they could influence its over-all price.

Examining these salient features of public land policy in the context of the determinants of economic growth, we might, on the face of it, expect them to have very little effect upon economic growth. While a system of land distribution by auction or by giving it away (under the Homestead Act) would certainly have consequences for the distribution of income, it is not obvious that such policies would have any striking effects upon the growth of the economy. These methods of distribution generally lead to efficient resource allocation.[16] This statement perhaps begs the issue, because the historian's implicit or explicit criticisms have been that some hypothetical alternative would have yielded a higher rate of growth. However, I know of no hypothetical alternatives, either explicitly advanced by historians or implicit in their criticisms, that would produce such a result.

One explicit hypothetical alternative that has been advanced is based on the contention that the unlimited amounts of land made available had adverse effect upon economic growth. Actually, just the reverse is true. The notion that limiting the amount of land made available would have accelerated growth is incorrect, since such action would have decreased the supply of productive factors from those that were, in fact, available. And since in this case the productive factor that would have been limited was land of superior quality, compared to that in production, any restriction would have had an adverse effect on the growth of the economy.

If speculators deliberately held land out of production (which should have had an adverse effect upon growth for the reasons just described), it would be surprising. The purpose of speculation is to make money, and by following a withholding policy, the speculator would have been doing just the reverse. That is, to the extent that speculators bought up great tracts of land and held them for appreciation, they were tying up large sums of money in the initial cost of acquiring the land and were foregoing income from that money used in another way—such as buying bonds. It would have been to their advantage, while holding the land, to rent it out, but buyers were easier to find than tenants. With so much land available free or at very low prices, a settler had an opportunity

---

[16] The exceptions to this statement are discussed farther on in this section, but the general conclusion is that a rather broad range of disposal policies, from the auction system to giving land away free, was consistent with a high rate of growth. Imposing a high minimum price, however, would have had adverse effects, for reasons discussed above.

for a windfall in acquiring land of his own, rather than renting or working as a tenant.

Land grants to railroads should have accelerated economic growth. First, railroad construction was consistent with improving the rate of growth. Second, this construction would have been slower, or in some cases perhaps lacking, without the land grants, because the private rate of return from railroad building was too low to encourage investors to put their funds to this use. Third, the land grants gave impetus to construction by permitting investors to share, through the appreciation of land values, in some of the social rate of return from railroad building.

Public land policies had few adverse effects on economic growth, none of them very significant, but four might be mentioned. One, giving away land under the Homestead Act probably encouraged some inefficiency by attracting to agriculture people who would have been more productive in other employments. Two, until the Graduation Act, large parcels of land were left idle because the potential capitalized income stream from them was lower than the minimum price set by the government. Clearly, the Graduation Act should have come in earlier, so that these lands could sooner have been put to productive use. Three, the unit of 160 acres set by the Homestead Act became increasingly inappropriate as available land dwindled to nonarable pasture land for which any efficient use would require much larger tracts. Admittedly, the ultimate result of this would be gradual consolidation into larger parcels of land as settlers recognized the facts; in the short run, however, and with the settlers' imperfect knowledge about agricultural and farming possibilities, it probably led to poor utilization of the land. Four, the alternate sections in railroad land grant areas —that is, those sections retained by the government to be opened up for homestead use—were held off the market for varying periods of time. It would have been a gain to national income to have opened up the settlement as rapidly as possible, since the sections were areas where the potential income was greatly enhanced by availability of lower cost transportation.

The broad, tentative conclusion to be drawn, therefore, is that subject to the exceptions just noted, land policies in general were consistent with a high rate of economic growth, and it would be hard to develop a hypothetical alternative that would be a very great improvement. These conclusions follow, however, only if the tentative hypotheses advanced above withstand empirical tests, and very little systematic work has given us evidence for testing. A study of Robert Fogel's, *The Union Pacific Railroad: A Case in Premature Enterprise*,[17] shows that the social rate of return on the land grant railroad, the Union Pacific, was extremely high and substantially higher than the private rate of return. In the years 1870 to 1879 the private rate of return was 11.6 per cent. The social rate of return, reflecting the increase in national income as a result of the increased value of land along the railroad, was 29.9 per cent for these years.[18] Clearly, in this case the social rate of return indicates that the railroad construction contributed to economic growth, and the land grants helped to increase the private rate of return to make it worthwhile to construct the railroad.

The major effect of public land policies was upon the distribution of income. Did they, as so many historians say, favor the rich at the expense of the poor? Without the necessary evidence, the following conclusions are tentative. First of all, giving away the land instead of selling it is a redistribution of income in favor of the homesteader and against the taxpayer (rich and poor): the government must get revenue from sources other than land sales, and the homesteader is getting a windfall in free land that has a positive value. Next, it is probable that large speculators did better than small ones. They were better informed, had better knowledge of the complex laws involving land disposal, had better knowledge of the possible alternatives, and—in a somewhat imperfect capital market—had better access to capital than the small speculator. We would expect, therefore, that their rate of return on investment in land would typically have been higher than that of the small speculator or of the individual settler. Third, the results of the railroad land grants are more uncertain. They added to the income received by the railroads, but the alternate sections retained by the government were ultimately put into the hands of settlers and farmers, to whom they brought windfall gains, the land's value having increased as a result of nearby, low-cost transportation.

[17] (Baltimore: Johns Hopkins, 1960.)
[18] *Ibid.*, pp. 96-103.

To the best of my knowledge, there have been no significant studies of the land disposal system's impact upon income distribution, exploring the rate of return received by large speculators compared to those of small speculators or settlers,[19] nor has any examination of land grants to the railroads disclosed their effects on income distribution.[20] If we had this information, we could compare it with the hypothetical alternative—which would be a system based on policies proposed by land reformers throughout the nineteenth century and implicit in many of the criticisms advanced by historians. The needed work is still to be done.

[19] A careful study by Allan and Margaret Bogue, "Profits and the Frontier Land Speculator," *JEH*, XVII, No. 1 (March 1957), shows a widely varied pattern of results in which some cases of relatively high rates of return were matched by other cases of low or negative returns, so that the general pattern does not appear to be one in which speculator profits were extremely high. It does not answer the question posed here, however, of the differential return of large versus small speculators. In a forthcoming article in the *Journal of Economic History* entitled "Land Speculator 'Profits' Reconsidered: Central Iowa as a Test Case" R.P. Swierenga provides evidence that large speculators in that area did enjoy very high rates of return.

[20] The recent review of the impact of the Homestead Act by Paul W. Gates suggests that at least until 1880 it did lead to the permanent acquisition of a sizeable number of homesteads that became operating farms. (Gates, in *Land Use Policy*, pp. 28-47.)

chapter 11

AGRARIAN DISCONTENT—
THE PLIGHT
OF THE FARMER,
1865-1900

Between the end of the Civil War and 1900, the agrarian sector of the economy was in a continuous state of turmoil and political unrest. A whole series of protest organizations and political parties evolved with the aim of improving the lot of the farmer, beginning in 1867 with the Granger Movement, which aimed at a variety of economic policies including railroad regulation and the formation of cooperatives. This was followed by the Greenback Movement, which focused on increased circulation of greenbacks as a means to a rising price level. Then came the Populist Party of the 1880's and early 1890's, with a variety of reform programs culminating in a demand for free coinage of silver as well as gold. In his distress, the farmer was attempting to initiate fundamental reforms in the American economy. While the movements varied in intensity over time and among the separate agricultural regions, they mirrored general dissatisfaction of the farmer with his lot. From his viewpoint, economic issues were central to the problems that he faced. But was his view accurate? Let us look carefully.[1]

The major complaints of farmers at that time, generally echoed

[1] I am indebted to Ray Lindstrom, whose paper on this subject presented in a senior class in economic history drew my attention to the material on mortgages in the Eleventh Census, and to my colleague Bob Thomas for our discussions of the problems.

by modern historians, were as follows: (1) The prices of agricultural goods had fallen more than the prices of other goods, and they had done so because other prices had been held up by monopolistic elements in the economy. The purchasing power of the farmer, therefore, was falling. For every bushel of wheat that he sold, he was able to buy less of the things he needed. (2) Railroads, grain elevator operators, and middlemen in general were using monopolistic practices to absorb all the profits from agriculture, rather than passing on to the farmer any of the gains accruing from improving transportation and improving organization of the agricultural market. (3) The usurious rates of moneylenders were robbing the

CHART 21. AGRICULTURAL TERMS OF TRADE, 1865-1890. RATIO OF FARM PRICES TO ALL PRICES. 1910-1914 = 1.0

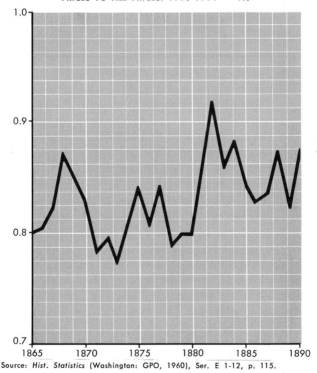

Source: *Hist. Statistics* (Washington: GPO, 1960), Ser. E 1-12, p. 115.

farmer. This was a complex complaint. The farmer—and subsequent historians—felt that the eastern capitalist and his western equivalent in mortgage companies were deliberately, by monopolistic practices, charging very high rates for loans to farmers, imposing a particularly heavy burden in a period of expansion when most farmers needed such loans. Moreover, in a period of falling prices, having a fixed debt was an even heavier burden, because the dollars to be paid back were worth more than they had been at the time when the debt was contracted.

Let us examine each of these complaints in turn. Take the first one: here, a comparison of the prices of farm commodities with those of all other commodities in the Warren-Pearson index fails to support the farmers' position. Chart 21 shows the ratio of farm prices to all prices (the agricultural terms of trade). The rising trend line is clear evidence that farm prices fell less than all prices during this period. Moreover, this evidence probably understates the "terms of trade" position of the farmer. If we compare the prices of farm products with those of specific manufacturing products, such as metal and metal products or textile products, we find that in each case the fall in the price of farm products was less than those in the manufacturing goods. Furthermore, while the quality of farm products changed very little (if at all), that of manufactured goods was steadily improving (which is not reflected in that price index). The farmer, therefore, was really getting more for his money.

Let us examine the second issue. Again the complaint is not supported by the available evidence. The fall in railroad rates during this period is striking.[2] It is true that railroad rates east of Chicago descend more strikingly than those of the "Granger railroads" west of Chicago; nevertheless, the dip in rates even west of Chicago is far greater than the general decline in the level of prices; as a result, the farmer was surely receiving additional benefits. Still another piece of evidence supports the general improvement of the farmer's position. A look at the spread between the Liverpool price and the price on the farm shows that over this period the divergence narrows strikingly; the farmer was now receiving an in-

[2] For a summary description of railroad rate falls, see Fred Shannon, *The Farmers' Last Frontier* (New York: Holt, 1963), pp. 296-97.

TABLE 17. PER CENT OF AVERAGE U.S. PRICE RECEIVED BY FARMERS OF WEST NORTH CENTRAL STATES					
	1911-15	1901-5	1891-95	1882-86	1871-75
Minn.	99	97	95	88	74
Iowa	98	94	95	85	70
Mo.	106	104	93	96	96
N. D.	97	90	82	81	—
S. D.	94	86	83	81	—
Neb.	93	86	83	73	65
Kan.	99	93	85	81	92

Source: L. B. Zapoleon, *Geography of Wheat Prices*, U.S. Dept. Agriculture, Bulletin No. 594 (February 21, 1918). Washington: GPO, p. 27.

creasing proportion of the total Liverpool sale price of a bushel of wheat. This is not surprising when we remember how much ocean freight rates and railroad rates fell during this period. Table 17 shows the critical part of this improvement—that is, the percentage of the average U.S. price received by the farmer. Since the ocean freight rate on wheat in 1900 was less than one-third the 1870 rate, clearly, the farmer's percentage of the Liverpool price had undergone dramatic improvement. Morton Rothstein summarizes the efficiency of the U.S. international grain trade as follows:

> With all its imperfections, it was the highly developed and tightly organized grain business, along with additional advantages in transportation, that accounted in large measure for the unique position of the American wheat trade in the last three decades of the nineteenth century. This is less valid for the important Pacific Coast trade, where there were no elevators and transport facilities were often comparatively poor. But east of the Rockies the business of assembling, handling, financing, and transporting grain was vastly superior to that of any other nation. Once American supremacy had been established, other countries sent a stream of official and quasiofficial missions to the United States to study the operation of the grain trade in the hope of emulating its efficiency. In most cases they sought to introduce the technology involved— such as grain elevators and systems of grading and inspection—but were anxious to forego the establishment of futures markets.

Yet futures trading, which was introduced into the grain trade by Americans and reached its highest development in the United States, was fundamental to the system as a whole. In spite of the almost universal condemnation of grain speculators it was this group which reduced many of the risks inherent in a free market. On the whole they endured heavy losses down to 1896 and made relatively modest gains from the rise in prices after 1897. By protecting millers, dealers, and exporters from losses, they helped to narrow the difference between the average price paid to farmers and the average price charged to the ultimate consumer.[3]

Next, let us take a look at the mortgage picture. A surprising feature is the small percentage of mortgaged farms in the U.S. as a whole. Approximately 29 per cent of the farms were mortgaged, to 35 per cent of their value. For the North Central area as a whole, where the complaints of the Populists were most vociferous, 38.7 per cent of the farms were mortgaged in 1890. The highest states were Kansas, with 60 per cent, and Nebraska, with 54 per cent.[4] Equally striking is the short life span of mortgages. The average life of a farm mortgage in 1890 was four and one-half years for the North Central area, while those of Kansas and Nebraska were 3.6 and 3.7 years respectively.[5] Since the mortgages were so short that no substantial changes occurred in the price level over those brief periods of time, a falling price level with a fixed mortgage imposed no great hardship on the farmer; and when he took out a new mortgage, he did so at a new rate.

The one place where there is some support for the farmer's position is in a comparison of mortgage interest rates in the North

[3] Morton Rothstein, "America in the International Rivalry for the British Wheat Market, 1860-1914," *The Mississippi Valley Historical Review*, XLVII (Dec. 1960).

For further statistical support see Holbrook Working, "The Financial Results of Speculative Holding of Wheat," *Wheat Studies of the Food Research Institute*, VII (July 1931), 405-38. On the narrowing of the difference in prices see Henrietta Larson, "Wheat Farmer and Market in Minnesota, 1858-1900," *Studies in History, Economics, and Public Law* (New York: Columbia Univ., 1926), CXXII, 243-56; and J. Chester Bowen, *Wheat and Flour Prices from Farmer to Consumer*, U.S. Dept. Labor, Bureau of Labor Statistics, Bulletin No. 130 (Washington, 1913), *passim*.

[4] "Real Estate Mortgages," U.S. Bureau of the Census, *Eleventh Census of the U.S., 1890*, p. 123 (Percentage of Farms Mortgaged).

[5] *Ibid.*, p. 109 (Life Span of Farm Mortgages).

Central area with those in the rest of the United States. The average rate of interest was approximately 8½ per cent for Kansas and Nebraska, and about 8 per cent for the North Central area as a whole, compared to 5½ per cent for the Atlantic area. While mortgage rates had fallen from as high as 10 or 12 per cent in the North Central area at an earlier date, it is likely that the capital market was still somewhat imperfect and that this imperfection worked against the western farmer in the sense that he did not enjoy as favorable rates of interest on mortgage loans as did the eastern farmer.[6]

These economic complaints do not appear to have been the fundamental causes of farm distress. True, it is evident that plenty of individual grievances were caused by monopoly power of the railroads, or by middlemen, or by imperfections in the capital market that allowed farm mortgage rates to be higher than elsewhere. *But had these specific situations been changed or modified anywhere along the line, the basic distress felt by the farmer would not have been alleviated.*

Its causes lay deeper. What was fundamentally at stake in the farmer's discontent was, first of all, that he found himself competing in a world market in which the fluctuations in prices made no apparent sense to him. The bottom might drop out of his income because of a bumper crop at the other side of the world, in Argentina or Australia. When he suffered a period of drought and poor crops, the higher prices he had learned to expect in such a case might still not be forthcoming (if other areas had a good crop year).

Let us examine in more detail what was happening to the agricultural sector during this period. First, the demand for major agricultural goods, particularly wheat, cotton, corn, and livestock had been growing rapidly. In general, it is true that the demand for agricultural goods is based primarily on expanding population; therefore, as the United States population grew, the demand for

[6] These come from *Eleventh Census of the U.S., 1890*, "Real Estate Mortgages," p. 259. Lance E. Davis makes a case for an imperfect capital market in "The Investment Market, 1870-1914: The Evolution of a National Market," *JEH*, XXV, No. 3 (Sept. 1965). However, it is hard to know how much of this was the increased risk of mortgages out on the frontier (see quotations in previous chapter) compared to loans on going farms in the East.

foodstuffs also grew rapidly. This domestic increase in demand was accompanied by a growing worldwide demand for agricultural goods, which the American economy was able to provide. Before the Civil War, the United States had been a major provider of cotton and, sporadically, wheat. But with the repeal of the Corn Laws in England in the middle of the nineteenth century and with the increasing industrialization, England became a major importer of wheat, and the United States became a major supplier of wheat for Britain and other European countries. Corn was primarily used to feed livestock; but livestock itself was in demand internationally, while cotton continued to be a leading American export throughout. Thus, it is obvious that the international market formed an important component of the growing demand for American agriculture. On the supply side, as already observed in the previous chapter, the westward movement opened up new land, and the development of transport media encouraged settlers to move into these areas in response to expected profitability. Thus, the vast western half of America was settled.

This is not the whole story of the supply-demand relationship, however. Concurrent with the westward movement in America and the consequent rapid increase in the supply of agricultural products, particularly wheat, other vast areas in the world were also becoming leading suppliers of this grain. Australia, Argentina, South Africa, the Ukraine of Russia, and even (for a while) India were all areas where a supply of wheat was evolving for the world market. In this competitive situation, nothing could prevent the price of agricultural commodities from fluctuating widely under varying conditions of climate and rainfall. A year of poor crops in the United States might coincide with bumper harvests in Australia, Argentina, and other parts of the world. As a result, the price of wheat would be depressed by oversupply, even though the share from western America was small. Similarly, it would be possible for the price to rise even with a bumper harvest in America if the reverse were true in other parts of the world. While the international market determined prices of wheat and some other agricultural commodities, many other agricultural foodstuffs and raw materials were limited to the U.S. market. The vast domestic market was also subject to sharp variations in supply and price.

Agriculture labors under another difficulty. In the long run, it tends to produce only low profits, because of its ease of entry. High prices induced a rapid expansion of agriculture and an increase in supply as people moved to new lands. But the resultant expansion tended to decrease prices so far that profits were vanishing, until readjustment took place and marginal producers moved out of that sector into more profitable occupations. This point needs to be stressed: a competitive industry is one in which the adjustment to low but positive profits is accomplished by producers readily moving into the industry when profits are high or moving out of the industry when profits are low. Obviously, agriculture meets this definition.[7] So it is far from surprising that in the last half of the nineteenth century, with surges of new farmers moving into the industry and a vast expansion of acreage under cultivation, lengthy periods of depressed prices resulted from the relative oversupply of produce—oversupply in terms of a price that would yield the farmer a normal profit.

In short, a vast process of worldwide adjustment was taking place in which the demand for agricultural commodities was growing rapidly, but the supply was growing in vast surges. Inevitably, there were times of high prices and above-normal profits countered by other times of very low prices and no profits at all. When deficient crops resulted from poor rainfall or other untoward conditions in any area, the outcome was still more catastrophic, coupling a low yield to lower prices. Aggravating the difficulties caused by wide fluctuations in the prices of agricultural commodities was the fact that prices in general were falling. This worldwide price decline resulted from a market economy's self-adjustment to two current factors: on the one hand, production and industrial output were expanding at a rapid pace; on the other hand, the money supply of the world, based on the amount of gold available, grew more slowly. More products competing for the same amount of money resulted in a striking fall in prices.

As though these woes were not enough for the nineteenth

[7] Although producers move into agriculture in periods of high prices, they do not as readily move out in periods of low prices, and the lag in response (while less critical in the nineteenth century when demand was increasing rapidly) became a critical factor in the twentieth century.

century farmer, this was the era when he was becoming a minority in America. Throughout all of our earlier history, his had been the dominant voice in politics and in an essentially rural society. Now, he was being dispossessed by the growing industrial might of America and its rapid urbanization. The farmer keenly felt his deteriorating status. His reading matter was full of warnings and complaints against the evils and moral decay of the city and its malign influence over the countryside. His disenchantment was an inevitable component of the vast and complex economic-sociological phenomenon that was taking place, involving both the commercialization of agriculture on a vast scale in a worldwide market and the farmers' becoming increasingly a minority group in American society.

WHAT HAPPENED TO FARM INCOME, 1865-1914

We lack good income statistics that would enable us to say with certainty what happened to farm income during this time of acute discontent from 1865 to 1896. The conclusion has often been that this was a continuous period of farmer distress resulting from falling farm income. Some of the evidence advanced above suggests this is not likely to have been so. Yet, it does contrast in striking fashion with the era 1896-1914, when there was evident prosperity in the farm sector, and the agitation of the farmer died down. One way to assess approximately what did happen to farm income is by taking a look at the value of land. Presumably, the value of land reflects the expected income that can be derived from that land; therefore, if land values were falling, this would provide evidence that farm income, too, was falling. Conversely, when land values are rising, the assumption is that farm income is rising too.[8] A recent study by John Bowman [9] carefully explores and examines land values in the Midwest during the period 1860-

[8] Actually, it is more complicated than this, since it is necessary to adjust for capital improvements, changes in the general price level, and application of the appropriate discount rate. Since "expectations" determine land values, it is assumed that these are derived from the past trend in land income.

[9] John Bowman, "Trends in Midwestern Farm Values, 1860-1914" (unpublished doctoral dissertation, Yale Univ., 1964).

1900, and the results suggest that farm income was rising substantially in the 1860's; that it was falling in the 1870's and rising again in the 1880's; and that it was roughly constant in the 1890's. Most interestingly, perhaps, the analysis shows that there was tremendous county-by-county variation in the relative income of farmers and that any broad picture obscures the degree to which this variation etched widely different patterns of prosperity among various farm groups in subregions of the whole area. The data that Bowman found are also supported by Bogue's study of the corn belt in Iowa and Illinois, in which he examines farm-mortgage foreclosure rates during these decades. The foreclosure rates in general suggest that the decade of the 1870's was indeed a period of real distress with foreclosure rates higher than in the 1860's, the 1880's, or the 1890's.[10] Although requiring substantially more research, this evidence does not fit the pattern of long-run continuous farm distress. Rather, it does suggest that there were periods of rising income interrupted by a very difficult decade of falling income in the 1870's.

There is no doubt that after 1896 farm income rose strikingly. It was a period of rising prices generally, but the prices of farm goods rose more rapidly than other prices. How do we explain the apparently erratic behavior of farm income before 1896 and the era of relative prosperity after 1896? A tentative hypothesis suggests itself from the following facts and empirical data: (1) Throughout the whole period 1865-1914 the demand for agricultural goods was increasing very rapidly. (2) Up until 1896 the increased supply of agricultural output came both from putting additional land of top quality into production and from increasing efficiency. (3) Between 1900 and 1910 the amount of new land put into farms increased less rapidly than in previous decades. In effect, the best land had already been taken up and put into production by that time, and the quality of the new land available was of lower yield. Between 1900 and 1914 there is little or no increase in total factor productivity in agriculture. Table 18, showing new land put into farms during the period 1870-1910, and Chart 22, showing total factor productivity, illustrate these trends.

[10] Allan G. Bogue, *From Prairie to Corn Belt* (Chicago: U. of Chicago, 1963), p. 179.

TABLE 18. NEW LAND PUT INTO FARMS, 1870-1914

Period		Thousand acres
1860-70		61.6
1870-80		134.9
1880-90	Yearly Average	55.6
1890-1900		117.2
1900-10		66.9
1910-11		19.0
1911-12		5.0
1912-13		7.0
1913-14		10.0
1914-15		11.0

Source: *Hist. Statistics* Ser. K 2, p. 278.

The tentative hypothesis is this: between 1870 and 1896, increased demand was met by surges of movement into new rich lands of equal fertility, resulting in low prices and productivity gains being passed on to consumers in terms of lower prices. As a

CHART 22. TOTAL FACTOR PRODUCTIVITY, 1869-1955
(Decade intervals 1869-1899; thereafter, 5-year moving averages)

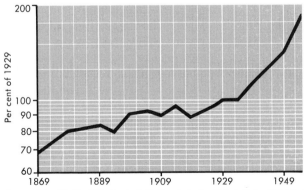

Source: John W. Kendrick, *Productivity Trends in the United States* (Princeton, N.J.: Princeton Univ., 1961), pp. 362-64.

result, the returns to farmers were generally low. After 1896, however, supply could be increased only by adding poorer land or more intensively farming existing land. Either way would raise the real costs of additional output, but it would also substantially increase returns for the best land in cultivation.

This explanation makes sense for agricultural commodities in the home market; nevertheless, it requires further explanation for commodities like wheat in the international market. If the hypothesis is universally true, new lands put into production after 1900 in Canada, Australia, and elsewhere must have been of inferior fertility to the best land put into production in the United States between 1865 and 1896.

chapter 12

CREATION OF
AN INDUSTRIAL GIANT
AND PROBLEMS OF MONOPOLY,
1860-1914

The Civil War was not a major impetus to accelerated industrial growth in America. This acceleration and the development of manufacturing had taken place before the war. But in the years from the end of the Civil War until World War I, manufacturing expanded so that the United States became the leading industrial nation in the world, with about one-third of the world's manufacturing capacity. The story of this industrial expansion is one of technological inventions fully exploited by entrepreneurs in an environment hospitable to such development. We can get a brief picture of this enormous expansion by looking at four cases that illustrate the combination of technological development with organizational ability responsible for this development.

Steel certainly played a pre-eminent role. Iron had been the primary material used, along with wood, in machinery and in most durable goods. Then, in the 1850's Henry Bessemer developed a process that (along with a similar development by William Kelly in the United States) revolutionized the use of steel. Superior to wrought iron, having much greater tensile strength and hardness, steel rapidly replaced iron in many uses (most important, in rails), as its price came down with the development of the Bessemer process. But quality control was difficult in the Bessemer process, and each batch of steel tended to vary. The open-hearth process, developed in the 1860's, was slower and initially more expensive; but because it enabled far better quality control and could make use of scrap, it gradually replaced the Bessemer process. Both methods originally could use only a narrow range of iron ores, excluding any with substantial amounts of phosphorus. The development of a basic lining that absorbed these impurities was a later, important development, first used in an open-hearth furnace in 1880.

Both the Bessemer and the open-hearth processes are most efficient when they are used in large-scale production; consequently,

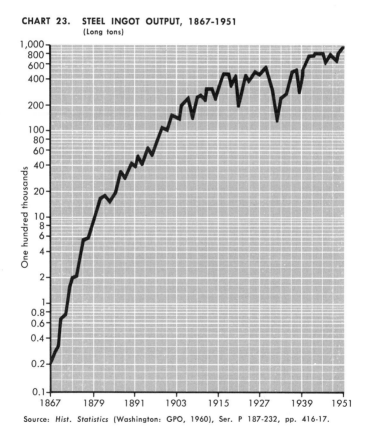

CHART 23. STEEL INGOT OUTPUT, 1867-1951
(Long tons)

Source: *Hist. Statistics* (Washington: GPO, 1960), Ser. P 187-232, pp. 416-17.

the new industry gradually developed large firms. In 1872, Andrew Carnegie launched the Carnegie Steel Corporation to manufacture steel rails. As time went on, he and his partners absorbed other firms and plants. In those days, the large amount of coal required to make steel (two tons for every ton of iron ore) led to the location of mills adjacent to coal fields. Carnegie combined organizational ability with access to the capital market and acquired or built successive plants to meet the expanding requirements of the steel industry. Other firms also developed. Chart 23 shows the rapid expansion of the steel industry as it rose from a mere 19,000 tons in 1867 to reach 10 million tons by 1900. As Andrew Carnegie is associated with the early developments of the steel industry, J. P. Morgan, financier, is associated with its giant consolidation and with the first billion-dollar corporation in the world. In 1901, Morgan pulled together all of Carnegie's properties, along with those of the other major steel firms in the United States, to form the United States Steel Corporation.

The story of petroleum is somewhat different. There were no awaiting markets for the sticky substance that oozed out of the ground in western Pennsylvania. It was regarded as a nuisance. Initially, interest was attracted to it for its possible use as an ingredient in patent medicine, and a number of eastern interests sent a "Colonel" Drake out to see what could be done. It was Drake who conceived the idea of pumping the oil out of the ground. Once out and refined, the middle-weight distillates such as kerosene became the main lighting source in America until they were replaced later by gas and electricity. The refineries built in the 1850's were small, costing little more than $400; but by 1880 a refinery cost $300,000, and by 1900, $1.3 million. As in the case of steel, the development of large-scale production and improvements in methods lowered the cost; the price of petroleum fell from 36 cents a gallon in 1863 to 8 cents a gallon in 1885.

Organization and development of the petroleum industry is inevitably associated with John D. Rockefeller. It was Rockefeller who consolidated the industry and initiated efficient, cheap transport methods, either by pressuring the railroads into developing them or by acquiring and developing pipelines for inexpensively carrying kerosene and other petroleum products to leading markets. Indeed, by the turn of the century, the Standard Oil Company had come to dominate the industry completely, and a new demand for petroleum products was appearing with the use of internal combustion in the new automobile.

The electrical industry, unlike steel, offers a case in which theoretical problems had been solved rather early—many of them by Michael Faraday. The industry was waiting chiefly for the development of a satisfactory dynamo; and in this invention, Thomas Edison played a leading role. Edison, virtually synonymous with the electrical industry—was an unusual combination in American history: he was an inventor, innovator, and often an entrepreneur. Like all entrepreneurs, however, even Edison made important mistakes. A serious error was his persistence in using direct current even while other growing firms were stressing alternating current as a more advantageous way of distributing and using electricity. Nevertheless, Edison developed a host of uses for electricity in which the electric light bulb and the whole system of electric lighting were critically important. The electricity industry became vital to manufacturing. The electric motor, especially designed for specific machines, made possible their more specialized and efficient use. Before Edison's time, an overhead belt had driven machines at a constant speed or at speeds varied by some system of reduction. An individual electric motor made it possible to turn off any machine or to operate each at a pace to match its particular function. Another development, the application of electricity to household appliances, continues even in the twentieth century as an industry of first-rate importance. Chart 24 shows the value of electrical appliances produced from the end of the nineteenth century until 1938.

The fourth industry is one that began at the end of the nineteenth century and has continued its major impact on the economy well into the twentieth century. This is the automobile. For a long time, man had been experimenting with various devices for gaining locomotion by some automatic power. One of James Watts' partners had been driving a steam-powered automobile at a very early date; and in the 1860's and 1870's in France and Germany, numerous experiments were underway with various kinds of automobiles and with the internal combustion engine, which ultimately became the main source of power. There was a long period of experimentation

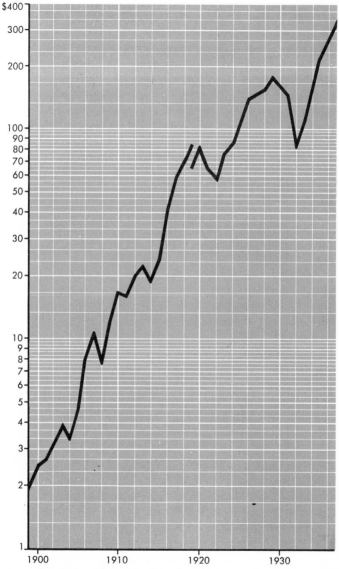

Source: *Hist. Statistics* (Washington: GPO, 1960), Ser. P 250-306, p. 420.

CHART 25. OUTPUT OF PASSENGER MOTOR VEHICLES, 1899-1938
(In millions of dollars)

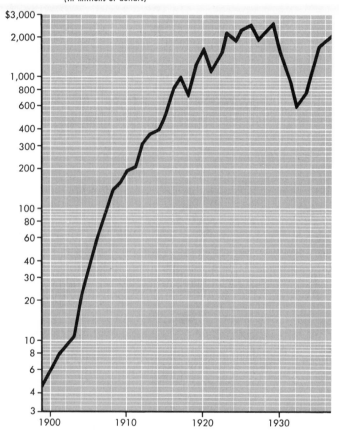

Source: *Hist. Statistics* (Washington: GPO, 1960), Ser. P 250-306, p. 420.

CHART 26.   INDEX OF MANUFACTURING OUTPUT, 1860-1914

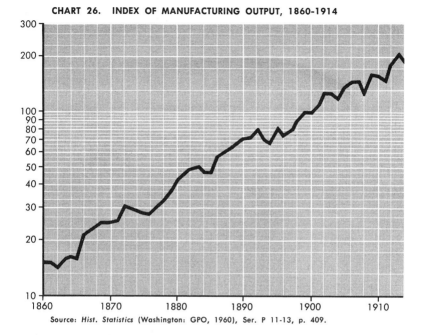

Source: *Hist. Statistics* (Washington: GPO, 1960), Ser. P 11-13, p. 409.

and debate about what kind of engine and fuel would prove most efficient. Should it be electric, or steam, or internal combustion? Even after this question was settled, there remained a period of adjustment in designing a body style that once and for all would disassociate the automobile from the carriage-without-a-horse concept.

Henry Ford took not new elements, but what were by then well established elements of the internal combustion engine, and combined them with a design that was definitely an automobile, not a horseless carriage. Then, using the ideas of Eli Whitney regarding interchangeable parts and mass production, he formed the assembly line. The net result was a cheap, mass-produced Model T, foreshadowing today's traffic jams. Chart 25 illustrates the spectacular growth of the automobile industry from its early beginnings in 1899, when only $4.2 million comprised the value of output, until 1919 when it passed the billion-dollar mark.

These brief case studies are illustrative of the dynamic changes in technology and in organizations in American industry. The results can be seen on Chart 26, which is an index of manufacturing output. Taking 1899 as the base year of 100, in 1860 the index showed only 16; by 1910 it had grown to 172, and by 1913 to 203.

What factors made possible this immense expansion? At the outset, it is necessary to separate two distinct aspects of this development: (1) the technological innovations that made possible the tremendous strides in industrial development, and (2) the special factors that made American manufacturing development increase at a rate greater than that in the rest of the world.

The technological changes described above were but a small sample of revolutionary changes in almost every type of manufacturing. The origin of these innovations was not confined to the United States; in fact, the bulk of them occurred in England, France, and Germany. Their development was accelerated by the rapid growth of scientific knowledge in the nineteenth century and by the rising incomes and rapidly expanding demand that characterized the Western world. But without a more refined exploration of the subject, a theory of technological change is still nonexistent.

The relative increase in the United States' share of the world's goods reflected the combination of rapidly increasing population and growing productivity that gave us a large share of the world's income. It is easy at this point to become involved in circular reasoning over (1) whether manufacturing development was responsible for rising income or (2) whether growing efficiency of the factors of production was the source of expansion; and manufacturing growth, using this new technology, was just one aspect of the development, given special impetus by the character of demand in this society (just as today's growing demand for services is leading to rapid expansion in that sector and relative decline in manufacturing). The second explanation is more consistent with the evidence of sources of productivity change. It is difficult to isolate particular attributes of manufacturing efficiency from the general increase in efficiency that characterized American society during this period. One general source was the size of the American market. A large population having relatively high incomes made possible all the potential economies of scale inherent in the technology of the individual industries.

An important initial influence was in the adaptation and modification of technology to fit American conditions (the relative prices of factors of production). The craftsmen, engineers, chemists, physicists, and other skilled members of the labor force were not just making use of existing equipment but were continually improvising and improving it as they went along, with the result that it is hard to distinguish the innumerable separate innovations that furthered development of each of the major industries. We tend to identify technological change with dramatic innovations such as the Bessemer process, but technical advancement was really an endless sequence of improvements made by unknown skilled and professional workers. This process reflected the quality of the labor force—the investment in human capital that distinguished the American work force—and the complementarity between human capital (engineers and scientists to make the essential modifications of technology) and physical capital (new or modified technology in the form of machinery, plant, and equipment).

American entrepreneurs are frequently singled out as the productive force that made possible the whole process. Their driving energy and often ruthless determination certainly led to new technology and its use in their large-scale organizations. Yet it is difficult to separate entrepreneurs from their environment and to credit the organizers with responsibility for this expansion. To the degree that certain extrepreneurial characteristics reflect the organizational skill learned in on-the-job training, credit goes to investment in human capital (in this case informal on-the-job training rather than formal education).[1]

Two other aspects of industrial growth should be mentioned. One has already been touched on—that America's labor supply was not purely indigenous, springing from the growth of our own population, but was augmented especially in the last half of the nineteenth century by sizeable immigration. More than a quarter of the popula-

---

[1] The spread of formal education was important in the improving quality of the labor force. Since it has been the subject of examination in previous chapters, it needs no further emphasis here.

tion of Pennsylvania at the end of the nineteenth century was made up of immigrants who formed a large part of the work force of the steel mills. Later on, they became an important part of the automobile industry work force.

The other major factor is the development of the capital market, and this requires more discussion. In the first chapter, we said that capital broadly conceived has a more useful definition than the narrow, traditional meaning. Nevertheless a further examination is needed of an efficient capital market, in the sense of organizing and channeling savings into the investments necessary to build factories and machinery, to clear and improve land, and to advance the working capital to maintain a labor force, inventories, and so forth.

While the focus here is upon the long-term capital market, it should be noted that in the years between the Civil War and World War I, the short-term market became more efficient.[2] The banking system expanded enormously in that period, both in the number of banks and in the amount of money in circulation. It was not until the very end of the period that any semblance of central banking re-emerged in America—a re-emergence from the long era of dispute following the end of the Second Bank of the United States, when Jackson vetoed its rechartering far back in the 1830's. With the Federal Reserve System, created in 1914, a central banking system was reconstructed, even though it was a decentralized one. However, the story of banking and the money supply properly belongs in a study of economic fluctuations and variations in the rate of utilization of resources—a subject to be explored in the next chapter.

The major concern here is with the evolution of the long-term capital market—that is, the evolution of a system of financial intermediaries that managed to get savings to flow into the industries that have been described in this chapter.[3] The growth of investment banking in America traces its heritage back to the need for large-scale capital financing for canals and railroads to the development of a regular connection between English investors who wished to

[2] Lance Davis, in his previously cited article, *JEH*, XXV, provides evidence of the reduction of interregional short-term interest differentials and therefore the improvement in the short-term national capital market.

[3] Another facet of the long-term capital market was the farm-mortgage market discussed in the previous chapter.

invest in American railroads and American financial institutions. Gradually, some of the investment banks, having started as branches of English firms, developed into primarily American houses. They became organizers of large-scale financing of major industries. Savings were held in trust and savings banks, insurance companies, and other repositories, and the investment banker formed "syndicates" of financial groups to underwrite the bond issues that went to build railroads, steel mills, agricultural machinery, and other major projects. The growth of these savings institutions and financial intermediaries led to the increasing efficiency of the long-term capital market.

Investment banking inevitably conjures up the name of J. P. Morgan and Company. This undoubtedly was the most famous of the investment banking firms, and one that exercised enormous influence over the development of financial markets in America. It was Morgan who more than anyone else was responsible for railroad consolidation in the latter part of the nineteenth century, and it was also primarily Morgan who organized a number of the more celebrated mergers and consolidations at this same time, of which the United States Steel Corporation was just one. If the investment banker performed the essential function of developing the long-term capital market and channeling the savings of Americans into industry, he also, by the end of the nineteenth century, posed a problem in terms of the growing consolidation of American business. This requires further examination.

As new industries developed in America and the pioneering firms made large profits, these high profits attracted new firms into the industry. The resulting competition lowered prices and frequently squeezed profit margins. It was not surprising that in the face of these declining margins, businessmen attempted to collude. The entrepreneurs mentioned in the brief illustrations above were cited for their contributions to organization of the industry; some of them are equally celebrated for their role as ruthless promoters of collusive activities. Sometimes this collusion was nothing more than a pooling agreement that lasted only as long as the members kept a good eye on each other. Gradually, however, more sophisticated techniques were developed. In the 1880's, the trust became the typical form of enforcing agreements. The trust placed the control of a number of firms in the hands of a single board of directors; thus, no individual company could take advantage of price cutting to beat out its competitors, and all operated as a unit. The widespread creation of trusts caused such immense public reaction that in 1890 the Sherman Anti-Trust Act was passed, making trusts illegal and outlawing other practices tending to monopoly. It was many years later, however, that the Act became effective. The Northern Securities case of 1904, dissolving a famous railroad merger between E. H. Harriman and J. P. Morgan, and the even more spectacular dissolution of the Standard Oil Company in 1911 showed that the Sherman Act did have some teeth.[4]

The era around the turn of the century probably represented the high tide of mergers, and indeed of monopoly, as reflected in organized control of major industries in the United States.[5] Most observers believe that since that time, monopoly—however defined— has declined somewhat in America. What accounted for the up- surge of mergers during that period? It is easy to explain why mergers were regarded favorably by business, for their part in eliminating competition and improving profits, and why they fre- quently were initiated by the investment banker who received a handsome reward for forming this consolidation; it is somewhat more difficult to explain the relative decline of monopoly in sub- sequent years. Some observers have put stress upon the Sherman Anti-Trust Act, subsequent acts such as the Clayton Act, passed in 1914, and more vigorous prosecutions by the antitrust division of the Department of Justice. Others have pointed to the success of new entrants into the field, who have continuously overturned major firms; and the failure of large firms to hold their position in the economy in the face of competition from new, young upstarts suggests that this has, indeed, been important. Still others point to rapid technological change which continually creates new, superior products to compete successfully with older ones. Whatever the

---

[4] A continuing problem for the courts was a good working definition of monopoly. Was it the percentage of the market that a firm controlled, the availability of close substitutes? Changing definition by the courts has led to changing policies.

[5] Since we know very little about the subject in the nineteenth century, this is pure conjecture.

causes, it does appear that the period at the turn of the century was the heyday for monopoly.

THE WELFARE OF THE WORKER
IN THE ERA OF THE ROBBER BARONS

In this era of aggressive industrial expansion, of the development of giant industries, and of entrepreneurs who have been labeled robber barons, what happened to the worker? Whether he was the immigrant coming over from the Old World or the farm boy leaving the farm to seek his fortune in the city, he found himself working in giant industrial firms and living in burgeoning cities filled with smoke, soot, poor sewage, and conditions that, from our present perspective, hardly appear favorable.

Working conditions in the big manufacturing firms, as well as the social conditions of the sprawling new cities, certainly left much to be desired. Yet we must note carefully that the implicit hypothetical alternative suggested by such a comparison is with today's society, with today's productive capacity—many times that of the turn of the century. The relevant hypothetical alternative does not implicitly suggest that the worker was exploited or that he experienced bad conditions by comparison with those of today; rather, it examines the extent to which the robber baron deprived the worker at that time. The lurid history of the aggressive entrepreneurs of the period leaves little doubt that they frequently robbed each other. How badly they victimized the worker, however, depended on the effectiveness of monopolies. The correct hypothetical alternative, therefore, is to examine what would have happened to per capita income in the absence of monopoly profits.

One of the costs of monopoly is in the misallocation of resources—that is, output is less and prices are higher than they would have been under competition.[6] More directly applicable to the issue we are exploring here, however, is a measure of monopoly profits at that time, on the assumption that this was income that under

[6] Arnold Harberger attempts to measure the misallocation costs of monopoly for the late 1920's in "Monopoly and Resource Allocation," *AER*, XLIV, No. 3 (May 1954), 77-87. His conclusion is that they are small, but much controversy has been generated by his assumption of long-run constant costs.

competitive conditions would have gone to the rest of the population. By reassigning these profits to the rest of the population, we can see how much difference they would have made to per capita income. We note that in the years 1900 to 1909, corporate profits before taxes were 6.8 per cent of the national income, which was approximately $20 billion at that time. This would make corporate profits about $1.4 billion.[7] If we take the figure $1.4 billion as profit and subtract from that the competitive rate of return on the non-farm reproducible capital in America—that is, the rate that capital would have earned had all the corporate enterprises been competitive—then the residual will be a crude estimate of the "excess" profits of monopoly. We find that the reproducible tangible assets that are nonfarm are approximately $20 billion;[8] and if we assume 5 per cent as a competitive rate of return, then $1 billion would be a competitive profit rate for society. This leaves a monopoly residual of approximately $400 million. If we redistributed this amount among the total population of 1905, the resultant addition to per capita income would be slightly less than $5 each. Average per capita income was about $250 in current prices at that time, so the addition would represent a 2 per cent increase in per capita income.

Although the above calculations suggest the income distribution effects of monopoly on the worker, a much more important issue is whether or not the worker was becoming better off at the turn of the century. A long-existing puzzle resulted from figures showing that not only in the United States, but in Britain and Germany as well, real wages of workers did not appear to rise very much between 1890 and 1914. The relevant study for the United States was one undertaken by Paul Douglas which indicated that real wages showed no rise for the period as a whole. This seems paradoxical in the face of the enormous expansion of output, and it did suggest that in the U. S., as in Germany and Britain, monopoly must have adversely influenced worker's real wages. However, a new study by Albert Rees, *Real Wages In Manufacturing 1890 to*

[7] There were probably some "monopoly profits" in unincorporated income, although not enough to influence significantly the figures used here.

[8] The actual figure for corporate reproducible tangible assets is $25 billion; however, I have allowed $5 billion for "watered" assets. This is certainly an overestimate of the extent to which this practice existed, but it serves to give an upward bias to the figure.

TABLE 19. AVERAGE HOURLY EARNINGS, ALL MANUFACTURING, 1890-1914
(Money and real terms)

	Average hourly earnings (current dollars)	Cost-of-living index (1914 = 100)	Average hourly earnings (1914 dollars)
1890	0.144	91	0.158
1891	0.144	91	0.158
1892	0.145	91	0.160
1893	0.151	90	0.168
1894	0.139	86	0.162
1895	0.138	84	0.165
1896	0.144	84	0.172
1897	0.140	83	0.168
1898	0.137	83	0.166
1899	0.146	83	0.176
1900	0.151	84	0.179
1901	0.158	85	0.185
1902	0.165	86	0.191
1903	0.170	88	0.193
1904	0.169	89	0.190
1905	0.172	88	0.194
1906	0.184	90	0.204
1907	0.191	94	0.203
1908	0.184	92	0.201
1909	0.186	91	0.203
1910	0.198	95	0.209
1911	0.202	95	0.213
1912	0.207	97	0.213
1913	0.221	99	0.224
1914	0.220	100	0.220

Source: Albert Rees, *Real Wages in Manufacturing, 1890-1914* (Princeton: Princeton Univ., 1961), p. 4. Copyright 1961 by Princeton University Press.

1914, under the auspices of the National Bureau of Economic Research, fundamentally revises this impression. Rees's figures show that hourly earnings adjusted by a new cost of living index rose significantly in the period from 1890 to 1914, as Table 19 indicates. Indeed, new findings on Germany also suggest that the original impression of constant real wages in that country during the period needs revision as well.[9]

While these findings cast doubt that monopoly either pauperized the worker or prevented the growth of real wages, they in no way modify the long-standing view of the social historian that there were serious costs to society and to the worker in the crowded tenements, slums, and ghettos that grew up in major industrial cities during this period. A neglected but important subject in American economic history is the analytical study of urban development and its attendant social costs.

[9] V. Desai, "Real Wages in Germany 1890 to 1914." Part of a study to be published by Oxford Univ. Press.

chapter 13

WAR, PROSPERITY, DEPRESSION, AND WAR, 1914-1945

Economic history of the twentieth century has been in marked contrast to that of the nineteenth. The nineteenth century was one of growing international interdependence, unequaled movement of peoples from Europe to the newly settled lands of the rest of the world, and a flow of capital to aid in their development. The spread of new scientific ideas as embodied in technology led to growth in many parts of the world. In hindsight it is frequently argued that in the nineteenth century, development was limited to a small part of the world; however, in comparison to anything in the past, it was a century of unprecedented development, one in which man, by and large, could optimistically envision a continually expanding future. In contrast, the economic history of the twentieth century has been dominated by two global wars and a depression of unequaled severity. They have led to fundamental reorientation of the economy, to a new role for government, quite different from any it had occupied before, and to a far-from-optimistic view about the prospects of the world, in spite of the fact that the promise of modern technology is vastly greater than it was at the end of the nineteenth century.

War involved mobilization of resources and their diversion from the end objective of satisfying consumers in a peacetime economy to the immediate objective of effectively prosecuting a war. It is not surprising that when a war ends, the economy faces basic problems in dislocation, in returning to the end objective of a consumer-oriented economy. During war, it is essential that a government control and direct the flow of resources for prosecuting the war; and when the war ends, the government tends not to release all of the controls. In 1919 with the end of World War I, however, the United States appeared well on its way back toward a consumer-oriented economy as demobilization took place on a substantial scale.

The first postwar cloud was the sharp, brief recession of 1921 —a recession sometimes called an "inventory recession" because it has frequently been argued that it was caused by a rapid accumulation of inventories which could not then be sold at existing prices. The result was a sharp fall in prices and very brief unemployment distress, but thereafter the 1920's were a period of relative prosperity, marked by substantial growth, rising real wages of the worker, growing incomes, and particularly, expansion of the consumer durable goods industries. This was the decade in which the refrigerator, the radio, the gas or electric stove, and most notably the automobile became a part of most households in America. Mass production and low prices put automobiles and other consumer durable goods within the reach of most families.

Yet the decade was not prosperous for everyone. Even while incomes were steadily rising and the worker in manufacturing was increasing his standard of life, the farmer was struggling through a period of extremely low prices. We have already observed that the years from 1896 to 1914 were prosperous ones, followed by even more prosperous times during World War I, when the United States fed not only our own nation and army, but also our allies. The result was that agricultural prices rose sharply and farmers were encouraged to expand production immensely. When the war ended, the demand was substantially curtailed, as European countries erected tariff barriers to protect their own agriculture, and America in turn stopped the flow of immigration. Consequently, the demand for agricultural goods was substantially less than it had been earlier, and prices fell to extremely low levels.[1]

---

[1] The demand for agricultural goods is income "inelastic"—that is, when incomes go up, people do not spend much more money on food. Therefore, an increasing demand for agricultural goods is primarily a result of more

In the latter part of the decade, still another distressing sign appeared. This was the speculation in the stock market. From 1927 on, and especially in 1929, the investors became convinced that not only was prosperity here to stay, but that profits could be quickly made by buying a stock that would be sold at a tremendous profit after it had been bid up by everyone else. It appeared that everyone entered the stock market to engage in such activities; and as they did, they continued to bid up the prices. Many speculators bought on margin, borrowing funds, so that with a very small amount of their own money they acquired large amounts of stock. This was fine as long as the stocks kept rising: they could pay off the money they owed and still have substantial profits. But if the stock fell, that was something else again. The stock market disaster in the fall of 1929 was of an explosive character. There appeared to be no bottom, and the result was that stocks fell to such depths that they wiped out a tremendous number of investors and left them heavily indebted. Between 1929 and 1933, approximately four-fifths of the total value of stock disappeared. Table 20 gives an indication of what happened to the stock market in this period and shows that the fall was so precipitous that it was not until the 1950's that stock prices recovered to the level they had been in 1929.

If the stock market was the trigger to this depression, it was certainly not the cause in a fundamental sense. The causes of depressions, and cyclical instability, are inherent in a free market economy. A market economy operates on the basis of the multiple decisions of consumers, savers, and investors. The producer plays a key role here, in that he must make decisions in advance with respect to buying his plant and equipment, buying raw materials, and employing workers, all before he receives any return. He is betting on what the demand will be for the goods he produces and, therefore, on what he will get in return. As a risk taker, he is willing to invest when expectations look bright. Conversely, if the economic barometer seems to be falling, he will batten down the hatches and curtail investment; and with the fluctuation in investment, so will income fluctuate in the economy: if businessmen do not invest, then income will fall, and this tends to have a cumulative

---

people. With immigration cut off, a major source of increasing demand was eliminated.

TABLE 20. COLLAPSE OF STOCK MARKET

Year	Month, Day	Dow-Jones Industrial Averages	
		High	Low
1925	November 6	159.39	
	October 14		99.18
1926	August 14	166.64	
	March 30		135.20
1927	October 3	199.78	
	January 25		152.73
1928	November 28	295.62	
	February 20		191.33
1929	September 3	381.17	
	November 13		198.69
1930	April 17	294.07	
	December 16		157.51
1931	February 24	194.36	
	December 17		73.79
1932	February 17	85.98	
	July 8		41.22
1933	July 18	108.67	
	February 27		50.16
1934	February 5	110.74	
	July 26		85.51
1935	November 19	148.44	
	March 14		96.71
1936	November 17	184.90	
	April 29		143.65
1937	March 10	194.40	
	November 24		113.64
1938	November 12	158.41	
	March 31		98.95
1939	September 12	155.92	
	April 8		121.44
1940	January 3	152.80	
	June 10		111.84

Source: Robert Rhea, *Graphic Charts: Dow-Jones Daily Stock Averages and Sales*. Privately published by permission of Dow Jones & Company, Inc., 1931.

impact. As less income becomes available, workers are laid off; and since they are laid off and are no longer able to buy more goods, the expectations of other businessmen who are investing look dimmer still, and they too curtail investments. This descending spiral keeps going.

The banking system can play, and indeed should play, an important role at this point. The ideal objective of monetary authorities, through their control and operation of the banking system, is to insure that in periods of declining expectations, the stock of money will expand and the cost of investing fall. That is,

CHART 27. UNEMPLOYMENT, 1921-1941
(In 10,000's and as per cent of civilian labor force)

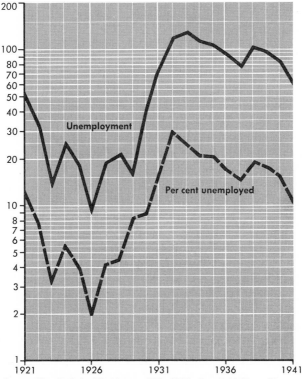

CHART 28. NATIONAL PRODUCT AND INCOME, 1921-1941
(Gross national product in $100 millions, per capita income in dollars)

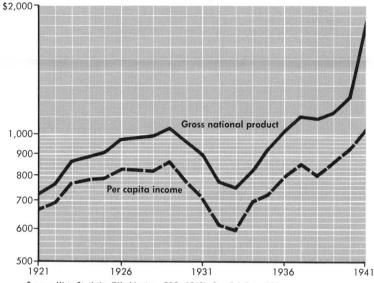

Source: *Hist. Statistics* (Washington: GPO, 1960), Ser. F 1-5, p. 139.

the objective of the banking authorities should be to attract investors at such periods; just as in periods of substantial inflation, the objective of the banking authorities is to discourage substantial expansion in the money supply and investing, in order to prevent rapid rises in prices when employment is full. The period from 1929 to 1932 is one in which the role of the Board of Governors of the Federal Reserve and their member banks has been severely criticized, because it does not appear today that the Federal Reserve did anything about the spiraling depression that was taking place. Their defenders have argued that in fact there was nothing that they could do, whereas the critics have maintained that the Federal Reserve never tried to do anything, although it had the power to increase member banks' reserves, thus expanding the money supply. Some critics have maintained that such a policy could have ended the Depression then and there. Whether or not this is true, it still is clear that the Federal Reserve was by and large passive during this period; and if anything, in September 1931 it further exacerbated the decline by raising the rediscount rate in order to prevent a gold drain.

The magnitude of the Depression can be judged from Chart 27, which shows the percentage of the labor force unemployed during this period, and Chart 28, which shows the fall in per capita and total incomes. A quarter of America's labor force was unemployed in 1932 and 1933. There was no precedent for such tremendous unemployment in American history. Moreover, they remained unemployed; and although gradual recovery was taking place, a very substantial share of the labor force continued out of work during the whole decade. It is not surprising in the light of the anomalous character of the Depression that the government should be confused about what to do.

Under President Hoover, a first effort was made towards recovery by setting up the Reconstruction Finance Corporation, developed by the government to make loans to encourage business to expand and develop in spite of the bad times. With $1.5 billion available, the RFC was a step in the right direction, but the amount was too limited to block the tide that was already swelling. A second effort was the Hawley-Smoot tariff act, raising tariffs but providing only some brief protection for some industries (in import-competing goods) at the expense of those engaged in exports. In order to help the farmer, President Hoover set up the Farm Board. Its objective was to stabilize farm prices, but the $500 million appropriated for this purpose was soon exhausted, and thereafter prices continued to tumble.

When Franklin D. Roosevelt came into office in 1933, the depth of the Depression had been reached, and he faced a new dilemma in the closing of the banking system throughout the country. His first hundred days were marked by an unprecedented series of legislative acts designed to get the country back on its feet, and his success with the banking system was one that inspired confidence in many people. Banks were audited, and those that appeared to be fundamentally sound were reopened with encouragement and support from the government.[2] His other legislation covered the whole gamut of activities of the New Deal, from set-

---

[2] After a four-day banking holiday, an emergency banking act was passed giving the RFC authority to support sound banks; and when banks judged to be sound were reopened, the fears of depositors were allayed.

ting up and establishing the Tennessee Valley Authority through the beginnings of the legislation toward social security. Let us first look at attempts to get out of the Depression, and then look at the other New Deal objective—reform.

Roosevelt's first effort to get out of the Depression was aimed at raising prices. The gold standard was abandoned, and gold was revalued, to encourage inflation. Next was the passage of the National Industrial Recovery Act. It permitted industries to collude and cartelize in order to raise prices and thereby give businessmen an incentive to produce. The Agricultural Adjustment Act (the heir of the old Farm Board) was designed to pay farmers to limit their production. It is easy in hindsight to see that these programs would not work. It would be hard to imagine that prices could be increased substantially in a period of such tremendous unemployment of resources or that industry collusion would encourage consumer demand. Nevertheless, they were groping and courageous efforts to stimulate the desperately ailing economy. The next efforts of the Roosevelt administration were aimed at what was called "priming the pump." In modern terms, this is called deficit financing; it is a system whereby the government spends more than it takes in tax receipts. Obviously, such spending on its own would tend to encourage expansion, unless it leads to curtailment of investment on the part of the private sector. Indeed, while Roosevelt was pragmatically experimenting with such activities. John Maynard Keynes was providing a theoretical justification for such spending in a revolutionary book in economics that advocated government deficit financing.[3] The problem with Roosevelt's "priming the pump" was that it was not enough and that the amount of deficit spending was so small that it was unable to lift the economy out of the depths to which it had fallen.

While the fundamental objective of the Roosevelt administration was recovery, a secondary one with lasting consequences was reform. A basic assumption underlying the operation of a market economy, badly shaken in the Depression, is that it operates in a way that provides maximum welfare for its citizens, and that no tinkering by government can improve upon this set of conditions.

[3] *The General Theory of Employment, Interest and Money* (New York: Harcourt, 1936).

Under the Roosevelt administration, this argument was swept aside in favor of one that maintained that governmental action could substantially improve the welfare of members of the society. Perhaps the most far-reaching of the legislation dealt with security for individuals. The security that once had depended upon close family unity was gradually disappearing in the face of the impersonal characteristics of an evolving market economy. The aged and the sick could no longer depend upon the family for security. Young people tended to underestimate what their needs would be in old age. A primary objective of a social security program was therefore to make provision for old age security from the beginning of employment. With this objective in mind, Congress passed laws on old age insurance, unemployment insurance, and workmen's compensation laws—all aimed at providing security for individuals under various kinds of duress and over various periods of their life.

A second area of reform was in securities and banking. The stock market crash as well as the failure of banks had convinced many that the underpinnings for each were faulty. The Banking Act of 1933 divorced investment banking from commercial banking, and the Securities and Exchange Commission was established to regulate the stock market. The Federal Deposit Insurance Corporation was set up to insure fully bank deposits up to $10,000 (and a percentage above that figure), and the Banking Act of 1935 was passed to expand the authority of the Federal Reserve Bank in monetary affairs.

While the federal government expanded the powers and increased the number of regulatory agencies trying to improve the performance of business, the Norris–La Guardia Act freed trade unions from the threat of injunction, and they were granted the right of collective bargaining first by section 7a of the National Industrial Recovery Act and subsequently as that provision was restated in the National Labor Relations Act of 1935.

A final area of government intervention was public investment in a variety of projects, of which the most noteworthy related to water resources. The Tennessee Valley Authority was established to develop an integrated multipurpose complex of dams for navigation, flood control, power, and recreation. In the Northwest, the Grand Coulee Dam provided power, but its ultimate objective was to irrigate a million acres of the Columbia Basin. The underlying assumption was that the gains to society from such activities—that is, social benefits—were greater than the private benefits and therefore were worthy undertakings, even if not privately profitable.

It is clear that by the end of the 1930's the role of government in the economy had changed fundamentally. Not only had it increased as a result of efforts to get the economy out of the Depression; it had increased also on the assumption that the welfare of the society could be improved by government intervention to reorganize and reallocate resources in particular areas, in contrast to the way in which the markets would have allocated them.

How successful was the New Deal in its efforts? Its success with respect to recovery was certainly far from complete. By 1940 a substantial share of the labor force was still unemployed, as the preceding charts show; this totaled 8 million people in 1940, comprising almost 15 per cent of the labor force, and 10 per cent were still unemployed in 1941 when the economy had begun to gird for war. The recovery that had shown promise in 1935 and 1936 was set back severely in 1937. Again, the policies of the Board of Governors of the Federal Reserve have frequently been blamed, in that they raised reserve requirements in the beginning of that year, so that the economy again fell back into the depths, re-emerging only by 1939. Certainly, the New Deal did not cause complete recovery, but an evaluation of its degree of success would have to be made against some hypothetical, alternative set of policies. One thing is clear, however: what the New Deal failed to do, World War II did with vigor. Between 1941 and 1942, when we suddenly became involved in global war, we again became a full-employment economy, remarkably illustrating how we could expand output and productive capacity and reorient ourselves to prosecute a war in a fashion and to a degree that amazed our allies and dismayed our enemies.

WAS THE NEW DEAL A SOCIAL REVOLUTION?

The New Deal provided hope and encouragement to millions in a desperate era. It equally produced violent epithets from businessmen and conservatives generally. Yet, viewed from a more detached perspective of more than a generation, what were the long-run consequences of the New Deal in terms of its effect on the welfare of American society? Was the New Deal really a new deal? Presumably, if it was, it (1) brought about a more fully employed economy, (2) accelerated the rate of growth of the economy, or (3) redistributed income in favor of that one-third of the nation who were ill-clothed, ill-housed, and ill-fed, to use Franklin D. Roosevelt's famous phrase. In order to do a careful appraisal, it would be necessary to spell out what hypothetical alternative we had in mind in each case. However, the necessary research has not yet been done, and at this point all we can do is to provide a more limited appraisal of the influence of New Deal policies.

With respect to full employment, we have already observed that the New Deal failed during the 1930's to accomplish its objective. Failure is not surprising in the light of governmental fiscal policy. A careful examination yields the conclusion.[4] (1) In only two years during the 1930's was governmental fiscal policy (at all levels) significantly more expansionary (in terms of its effect on aggregate demand) than it had been in 1929. The two exceptions were 1931 and 1936, when large payments to veterans were made over the objection of both the Hoover and the Roosevelt administrations. (2) Federal government fiscal policies were somewhat more expansionary (in part as a result of the veterans' payments, opposed by the executive branch) than state and local government policies; and when all three are taken together, they about cancel each other out in terms of any significant net effect. (3) The primary reason for this ineffectiveness was that taxes at every level of government expanded. All governments combined had run a deficit (spent more than they took in in taxes) in 1929, but from 1933 to 1939 (except 1936) all governments either ran a surplus (took in more than they spent) or had an approximately balanced budget.

Yet, the New Deal left one heritage that appears to have played an influential part in maintaining high levels of employment and income in periods of subsequent recession. These are the social security measures of old-age and survivors' insurance, unemploy-

[4] E.C. Brown, "Fiscal Policy in the 'Thirties: A Reappraisal," *AER*, XLVI, No. 6 (Dec. 1956).

ment insurance, and workmen's compensation. In periods of recession, they have maintained the income of unemployed workers and tended to limit the fall in income and to prevent the vicious spiral results described earlier. Social security measures appear to have developed some important, built-in stabilizers for mitigating subsequent recessions.

Did the New Deal affect the over-all growth rate of the economy? There is certainly no clear evidence on this subject. One would expect that New Deal measures that might have had some effect were (1) setting up regulatory bodies designed to improve the performance of business, with the result, presumably, of improving resource allocation, and (2) undertaking projects in areas where public investment might be assumed to have a higher social rate of return than private rate of return. Certainly, however, the results in both cases are equivocal at best. The regulatory bodies at times may have accomplished some improvements in resource allocation and industry performance; at other times, they proved to be handmaidens to the industries themselves, making unwise resource allocation and hampering rather than benefiting the performance of the industry. A continuing dilemma of regulatory agencies is that they can become vehicles whereby the regulated regulate the regulators, in the interest of the regulated—rather than that of the public.

I know of no over-all appraisal of government investment in water resources during the New Deal period. Perhaps the most important contribution was the impetus it gave to developing benefit-cost analysis, so that we could measure the rate of return on such projects and eventually extend our analysis to other types of government activity.

In many respects, the third issue was the one around which New Deal policy at the time became most controversial: the redistribution of income in the United States. For if the New Deal did not achieve full employment and if its implication for growth are at best equivocal, then the only way in which it could have benefited that one-third of the nation was by redistributing income in their favor, and it was clearly evident that the New Deal intended such results in a number of its policies. Specifically, policies that were aimed at encouraging the growth of trade unions—such as the

National Labor Relations Act and the Norris-LaGuardia Act—had the objective of expanding unionism in America, and it was comonly assumed unions would thereby increase incomes going to labor. These acts, together with the rivalry which developed between the American Federation of Labor and the newly created Congress of Industrial Organizations, did expand trade union membership from about 3 million in 1932 to 9 million in 1940. Similarly, the Fair Labor Standards Act, establishing minimum wages for workers, aimed at benefiting the lowest-income groups. The price-support program in agriculture, the subsidized low-cost housing for low-income groups, and the social security program were all aimed in this direction. What were their results?

Chart 29 shows disposable income of the top 1 per cent and

CHART 29. PER CENT SHARES OF DISPOSABLE INCOME RECEIVED BY TOP 1 PER CENT AND 5 PER CENT OF TOTAL POPULATION, 1919-1946

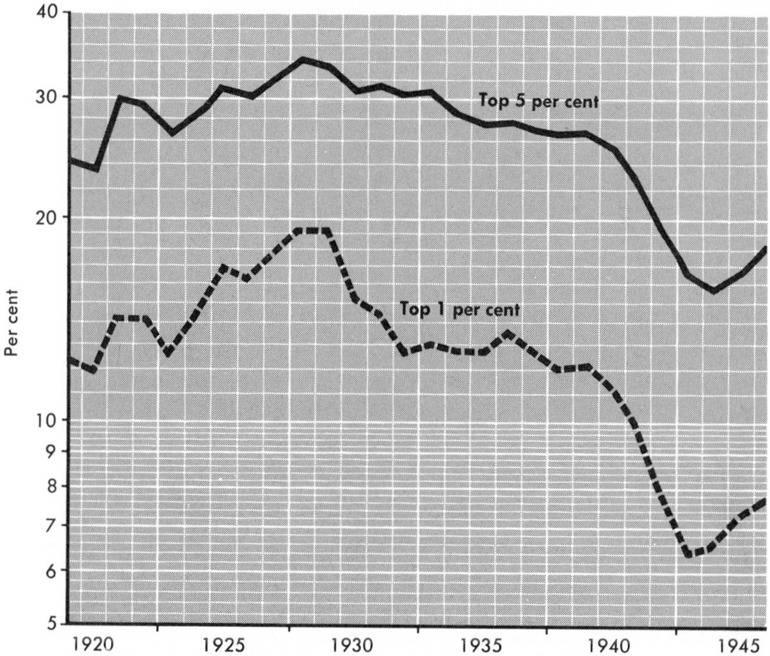

Source: *Hist. Statistics* (Washington: GPO, 1960), Ser. G 131-46, p. 167.

CHART 30. SHARE OF PERSONAL SECTOR WEALTH HELD BY TOP WEALTH-HOLDERS, SELECTED YEARS, 1922-1956

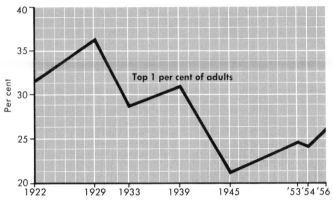

Source: Robert J. Lampman, *The Share of Top Wealth-Holders in National Wealth, 1922-56,* A Study by the NBER (Princeton, N.J.: Princeton Univ., 1962), p. 25. Copyright 1962 by Princeton University Press.

top 5 per cent of income groups between 1919 and 1946, and Chart 30 shows the share of the top 1 per cent of wealth-holders in the United States. Both charts show that wealth and income were becoming more unequally distributed in the 1920's, and both show that after 1929 the percentage of wealth and income of the top holders falls. The wealth picture shows that in the period 1933 to 1939, wealth-holding again became somewhat more unequal, although the income chart shows that the share of the top income-holder continues to fall throughout. The significant decline in inequality comes in the war years, however. It is equally evident that after the war, wealth and income again became somewhat more unequally distributed. During the Thirties, there was a decline in the share of the highest-income groups, but it appears to have gone to middle-income groups. The lowest 20 per cent of consumer units, in terms of their income, received 4.1 per cent of total family personal income in 1935; they received 5 per cent in 1947 and 4.6 per cent in 1962.

In summary, it is not at all clear that New Deal measures provided any significant redistribution of income. The fall in the share of top wealth- and income-holders came about as a result of the Depression in 1929, and there had already been a significant decline by the time the New Deal started. The really significant fall is clearly related to the high progressive tax rates imposed during World War II. Moreover, the redistribution from the very rich appears to favor middle-income rather than lowest-income groups.

A careful examination of the measures designed to effect this income redistribution suggests that this over-all result is not surprising. If incomes were being redistributed in the 1930's, it was because the laws that were passed either facilitated a relative rise in the low-income group or transferred income from higher-income groups to low-income groups. Minimum wage laws and promotion of trade unions were aimed at facilitating a relative rise in the low-income group, but their effectiveness in redistributing income in favor of low-income groups is debatable. It is not at all self-evident that minimum wage laws really raised wages of low-income groups. To the extent that they are effective, and that the minimum wage exceeds the value of output of workers, the long-run result will be more unemployment and therefore more inequality in income. Similarly, even though trade unions may raise wages of their members, it is a much debated point whether they raised wages over all. Labor's share of national income appears to have been increasing, but this is certainly not attributable to trade unions.[5] Therefore, if trade unions do manage to raise their wages but do not influence labor's share of national income, then they do so at the expense of three-quarters of the labor force, which is unorganized.[6] Since this includes most of the lowest-wage earners, the result appears likely to have made incomes more unequal, rather than more equal.

More effective results surely stem from the direct transfers of

[5] Labor's share of national income appears to have been increasing since about 1910, long before trade unions had any appreciable effect on the economy. A partial explanation is in the shift out of agriculture (self-employed entrepreneurial income) into wage status; but this is not a complete explanation. See Irving B. Kravis, "Relative Income Shares in Fact and Theory," *AER*, XLIX, No. 5 (Dec. 1959), 917-49.

[6] The impact of trade unions upon wages has been the subject of extensive inquiry. A recent study by H.G. Lewis (*Unionism and Relative Wages in the United States: An Empirical Enquiry.* Chicago: Chicago Univ., 1963) summarizes previous studies along with the author's own investigations. The result is an indispensable study for those who wish enlightenment on this controversial issue.

income from high to low-income groups, as in the case of public housing and welfare payments. Their magnitude in the Thirties does not appear to have been significant, although the slight increase in the position of the lowest quintan of income earners in the 1940's suggests that the highly progressive tax rates combined with welfare measures in that decade temporarily improved the status of the lowest-income group. But that modest result came after the New Deal.

chapter 14

CURRENT
ECONOMIC PROBLEMS
IN HISTORICAL PERSPECTIVE,
1945-1965

Economic problems of modern times have deep historical roots; few are really new. Let us look at some of the more important ones and their historical antecedents. The ending of World War II brought immense problems of economic readjustment—just as the Revolutionary War did, the War of 1812, the Civil War, and World War I. Any war commits the resources and manpower of a society and redirects them away from their previous uses into the essential military requirements. At the end of any war, the whole process must somehow be reversed to permit the market economy to get back into gear again, and to allow consumer wants again to dominate the pattern of output of goods and services. This was the condition of America in 1945, but still fresh in people's minds was the decade of depression that had preceded the war. Most economists predicted that the years following the war would again see substantial unemployment, and Americans were determined to avoid this consequence. Their determination was embodied in the Employment Act of 1946, deliberately making full employment a concern of the federal government. The act set up a Council of Economic Advisors to advise the President on measures to pursue in maintaining a full-employment economy. There was certainly nothing new about depressions in the American economy. Following the War of 1812, a depression began in 1818 and lasted until 1822 or 1823. One of the most severe depressions in American history began at the end of the 1830's and stretched until 1845. Others came in 1857, 1873, 1893, and 1907. It has already been noted that fluctuations in employment, typical of our economy in the past, are endemic to a market economy. The monetary controls of the federal government through the Federal Reserve System and the Treasury have grown over time, giving it a greater command over fiscal and monetary policies. It should also be noted, however, that the growing size of government as a percentage of total economic activity has given the government much more leverage in its influence upon full employment. One consequence of the New Deal observed in the previous chapter was that a variety of social security measures passed in the Thirties tended to even patterns of income over the business cycle. The results between 1945 and 1965 have been rather successful. There have been no major lapses from full employment, no depressions—only recessions in which the level of unemployment has been small, compared to those of previous eras. Nevertheless, as time has gone on, a stubborn phase of the problem has emerged. Beginning about 1957, levels of unemployment higher than might have been expected have continued to exist, even in good times. This level of unemployment has exceeded 6 per cent a good part of the time and has been above 5 per cent throughout. Part of the problem stems from the changing kind of labor needed in our economy. Increasingly, unskilled labor has been in declining demand, whereas skills and high levels of training have been in growing demand, leaving many unskilled workers unemployed. This is combined with the fact that some industries have been dying out, as in the case of the coal mines of Appalachia. There has been immobility of the people in moving out of those areas or in developing new skills for new jobs. But part of the problem also represents a continuing dilemma of a government faced by multiple issues. At the same time that the federal government has been concerned about unemployment, it has also been concerned about rising prices and about the outflow of gold from the U.S. economy.[1]

[1] An oversimplified explanation of a complex problem is that with fixed exchange rates, Americans want to buy more from foreigners than foreigners want to buy from us. The difference is made up by gold flows.

As a result, it has pursued a policy of deliberately allowing some slack in the economy, in order to prevent rising prices and rising interest rates that could lead to further outflow of gold. This highly controversial policy reflects a deliberate decision to trade off one set of goals against others and illustrates the dilemmas of current government policy.

Still another current economic problem has been of perennial concern and is a central theme of this book—the rate of growth of the American economy. Improving technology, more efficient economic organization, and increasing investment in human beings has resulted in a secularly rising level of well-being of the American society ever since it has been possible to measure growth. But in recent times, and particularly in facing the challenge of other economies, it has been frequently asked whether this growth could not be improved. Could the rate at which productivity has increased be raised? By doing so, would it be possible to increase the over-all growth rate from 3 per cent to 4 per cent? A moment's reflection would suggest that this is rather difficult to do. It is not just an increase of 1 per cent being contemplated; rather it represents an increase of one-third or 33 per cent of the growth rate, and a careful examination of the sources of growth suggests that this would involve substantial cost in other directions.[2] It is probable, too, that we are understating America's current growth rate, owing to some fundamental statistical problems in measurement. For one thing, as Americans have become richer, they have increasingly changed the direction of their buying habits into two areas of purchases that defy accurate measurement—services and goods—and in which there has been significant quality change. In the case of services, it is difficult to measure improved productivity. Take medical services for example. It is well known that tremendous improvement in medical knowledge has taken place in the last hundred years, but we have not found a satisfactory way to measure output and thereby measure output per unit of input, as we do with other kinds of activity. Consequently, for this as well as all other services, we simply do not measure the productivity change that takes place. As

---

[2] For a discussion of the issues, see E.W. Dennison, *The Sources of Economic Growth in the United States,* Supplementary Paper No. 13 (New York: Committee for Economic Development, 1962).

services become a bigger and bigger component of our national income, they become a more and more serious problem of understatement. Still another problem is the measurement of change in the quality of goods, a change that has occurred in most consumer (and producer) goods. Accuracy has not been possible in incorporating this quality change in productivity measures. Since a primary objective of modern business firms has been to improve the quality of goods in order to tempt consumers, the omission is serious. We are familiar with the fact that an automobile, a tire, a refrigerator, or a TV set is radically different from one of ten or fifteen years ago. But how do we measure this quality change in our index of changing efficiency? To measure a car of 1925 as equivalent to a car of 1965 is certainly an understatement both of efficiency change and of the satisfaction to consumers in the economy. These dilemmas of measuring the real growth rate are so serious that some of them probably cannot be solved, but with others we may hope to get at least some notion of the magnitudes involved and thereby gain a more accurate estimate of the rate of growth.

The problem of the gold drain and the balance of payments reflects America's international economic relations today. Viewed in historical perspective, they have changed radically over the past several centuries, but their influence has been a pervasive one throughout. In Colonial times, America's relationship with Britain was the most important influence on economic welfare. Later, when we became independent, important supplements to small local markets were made possible by the ability to trade with foreigners. The French and Napoleonic Wars became a significant period of accelerated growth as the United States took advantage of these markets. In the first half of the nineteenth century, overseas trade in cotton was a source of growing interdependence of the several regional economies in the United States. Immigration and the inflow of capital continuously added to the productive factors and thereby to extensive growth. In the twentieth century, the United States' international economic relations are obviously changing. The flow of international capital has reversed; the flow of immigration, upon which depended an important part of the expansion of population in the nineteenth century, was cut off after World War I; and foreign trade, although it represented a relatively small portion of

American national income, has become of tremendous importance to foreign countries. Still another aspect of international economic relations that has become important since World War II has been our attempt to raise the living standards of underdeveloped countries. American grants and loans since World War II have exceeded $100 billion. On top of this, private capital has also invested abroad at a very substantial rate. Indeed, it is the combination of the dollar's central position in world international monetary affairs, along with our foreign commitments, that is responsible for the gold drain and its attendant problems. The interdependence among major economic problems continues to exist in America as it has throughout our history.

These three current economic issues of full employment, economic growth, and international economic relationships illustrate one central aspect of our modern economy: the important role that government has come to play. Tables 21 and 22 illustrate the growth of government expenditures and finance. At the very start of our nation, government finances were a little over $4 million, and they grew slowly throughout the next decades. Although, as we know, the government did invest in a variety of economic activities, the results were probably rather modest in terms of their impact on the growth of the economy. The major changes in the rate and level of government expenditures had been brought about by war. War from 1860 to 1865, from 1914 to 1917, and then again from 1940 to 1945 had major impacts upon increasing government expenditures. The other chief source of increase was the Depression of the 1930's. Table 22 shows just how and where governments at all levels—local, state, and federal—have spent their money. Beginning in 1902 with a mere $1.6 billion, it soars to a 1962 figure of $176 billion. The biggest increase, as indicated, is in national defense, comprising the cost of past and current wars and preventive armament. Education, too, has increased immensely over this period, and the continuous efforts toward farm stabilization and raising the farm income have led to mounting expenditures.

There is wide difference of opinion among Americans, as indeed there has been throughout our history, about the proper role of government. This ideological difference has tended to becloud the issue—at least in economic terms. Careful, scientific assessment of

TABLE 21. EXPENDITURES OF THE FEDERAL GOVERNMENT, 1789-1964

(In thousands of dollars)

Year*	Total†	Year	Total	Year	Total
1789-91	4,269	1823	14,707	1855	59,743
1792	5,030	1824	20,327	1856	69,571
1793	4,482	1825	15,857	1857	67,796
1794	6,991	1826	17,036	1858	74,185
1795	7,540	1827	16,139	1859	69,071
1796	5,727	1828	16,395	1860	63,131
1797	6,134	1829	15,203	1861	66,547
1798	7,677	1830	15,143	1862	474,762
1799	9,666	1831	15,248	1863	714,741
1800	10,786	1832	17,289	1864	865,823
1801	9,395	1833	23,018	1865	1,297,555
1802	7,862	1834	18,628	1866	520,809
1803	7,852	1835	17,573	1867	357,543
1804	8,719	1836	30,868	1868	377,340
1805	10,506	1837	37,243	1869	322,865
1806	9,804	1838	33,865	1870	309,654
1807	8,354	1839	26,899	1871	292,177
1808	9,932	1840	24,318	1872	277,518
1809	10,281	1841	26,566	1873	290,345
1810	8,157	1842	25,206	1874	302,634
1811	8,058	1843	11,858	1875	274,623
1812	20,281	1844	22,338	1876	265,101
1813	31,682	1845	22,937	1877	241,334
1814	34,721	1846	27,767	1878	236,964
1815	32,708	1847	57,281	1879	266,948
1816	30,587	1848	45,377	1880	267,643
1817	21,844	1849	45,052	1881	260,713
1818	19,825	1850	39,543	1882	257,981
1819	21,464	1851	47,709	1883	265,408
1820	18,261	1852	44,195	1884	244,126
1821	15,811	1853	48,184	1885	260,227
1822	15,000	1854	58,045	1886	242,483

* From 1789 to 1842, years end December 31. From 1844 to 1964, years end June 30. Figures for 1848 are total for January 1 to June 30.

† Prior to 1930, includes tax refunds paid and capital transfers for wholly owned government corporations; thereafter, excludes them.

TABLE 21 (cont.)

Year	Total	Year	Total	Year	Total
1887	267,932	1913	724,512	1939	8,858,458
1888	267,925	1914	735,081	1940	9,062,032
1889	299,289	1915	760,587	1941	13,262,204
1890	318,041	1916	734,056	1942	34,045,697
1891	365,774	1917	1,977,682	1943	79,407,131
1892	345,023	1918	12,696,702	1944	95,058,708
1893	383,478	1919	18,514,880	1945	98,416,220
1894	367,525	1920	6,403,344	1946	60,447,574
1895	356,195	1921	5,115,928	1947	39,032,398
1896	352,179	1922	3,372,608	1948	33,068,709
1897	365,774	1923	3,294,628	1949	39,506,989
1898	443,369	1924	3,048,678	1950	39,617,003
1899	605,072	1925	3,063,105	1951	44,057,831
1900	520,861	1926	3,097,612	1952	65,407,585
1901	524,617	1927	2,974,030	1953	74,274,257
1902	485,234	1928	3,103,265	1954	67,772,353
1903	517,006	1929	3,298,859	1955	64,569,973
1904	583,660	1930	3,440,269	1956	66,539,776
1905	567,279	1931	3,577,434	1957	69,433,078
1906	570,202	1932	4,659,203	1958	71,369,000
1907	579,129	1933	4,622,865	1959	80,342,000
1908	659,196	1934	6,693,900	1960	76,539,000
1909	693,744	1935	6,520,966	1961	81,515,000
1910	693,617	1936	8,493,486	1962	87,787,000
1911	691,202	1937	7,756,021	1963	92,684,000
1912	689,881	1938	6,791,838	1964	97,684,000

Sources: For 1789-1957, *Hist. Statistics,* Ser. Y 350-56, pp. 718-19. For 1958-1964, *Statistical Abstract of the United States* (Washington: GPO, 1965), p. 392. (Figures rounded off to nearest million.)

TABLE 22. FEDERAL, STATE, AND LOCAL GOVERNMENT EXPENDITURE, BY FUNCTION, 1902-1962

(In millions of dollars)

Year	Total expenditure	National defense	Education	Highways	Public welfare	Stabilization of farm prices and income
1902	1,660	165	258	175	41	——
1913	3,215	250	582	419	57	——
1922	9,297	875	1,713	1,296	128	——
1927	11,220	616	2,243	1,819	161	——
1932	12,437	721	2,325	1,766	445	——
1934	12,807	553	2,005	1,829	979	382
1936	16,758	932	2,365	1,945	997	602
1938	17,675	1,041	2,653	2,150	1,233	326
1940	20,417	1,590	2,827	2,177	1,314	694
1942	45,576	26,555	2,696	1,765	1,285	929
1944	109,947	85,503	2,805	1,215	1,150	1,532
1946	79,707	50,461	3,711	1,680	1,435	2,012
1948	55,081	16,075	7,721	3,071	2,144	592
1950	70,334	18,355	9,647	3,872	2,964	2,712
1952	99,847	48,187	9,598	4,714	2,830	638
1953	110,054	53,583	10,117	5,053	2,956	2,271
1954	111,332	49,265	11,196	5,586	3,103	3,963
1955	110,717	43,472	12,710	6,520	3,210	3,892
1956	115,796	42,680	14,161	7,035	3,185	4,926
1957	125,463	45,803	15,098	7,931	3,453	4,980
1958	134,931	46,127	16,836	8,702	3,866	4,339
1959	145,748	48,389	18,119	9,726	4,193	5,858
1960	151,288	47,464	19,404	9,565	4,462	4,862
1961	164,875	49,387	21,214	9,995	4,779	7,331
1962	176,240	53,225	22,814	10,508	5,147	7,910

Sources: For 1902-1957, *Hist. Statistics*, Ser. Y 412-45, p. 723. For 1958-1962, *Continuation of Hist. Statistics*, 1965, p. 99.

the effectiveness of actual government policy in improving the economy and the general welfare must be compared to a hypothetical alternative. That alternative would be the economy's performance and consequent welfare in the absence of such government activity. Least controversial, perhaps, is government's role in maintaining a full-employment economy, although even here the policies that the government pursues frequently represent a compromise between full-employment objectives and other competing objectives. Much more controversial have been governmental policies related either to improving the performance of the economy in the long run (and this implies its influence upon economic growth) or to improving the welfare of individual groups, particularly low-income groups, in the economy. Some part of the controversy rests upon fundamental differences of opinion about the function of government, but a major part remains unsettled simply because the effectiveness of public policy has not been appraised in scientific terms.[3] It is true that in the area of governmental investment in water resources, such research has begun with benefit-cost analysis to measure the effectiveness of public policies; but only recently have economists begun to extend this type of analysis to other areas concerned with government policies. Clearly, benefit-cost analysis and similar techniques must be extended to appraise the effectiveness of public policy in all those other areas and to judge whether in fact they achieve their objectives better than alternative hypothetical policies would.

POVERTY IN THE MIDST OF PLENTY

A recurring concern of Americans throughout our history has been poverty. This concern differentiates us from most societies in the world, in that poverty has usually been taken for granted, much as it was in the days of Malthus, who assumed that we could never be rid of it. But in a society of growing affluence, poverty remains and becomes more and more of an anomaly. In periods when our

[3] In his presidential address before the American Economic Association in 1964, George Stigler emphasized this neglect and went on to point up the promise of modern methods of quantitative analysis in remedying this oversight. "The Economist and the State," *AER,* LV, No. 1 (March 1965), 1-18.

TABLE 23. PER CENT OF CONSUMER UNITS WITH
LESS THAN $3,000 INCOME
In 1954 dollars, in selected years
(National Income Division definition)

Year	Per cent	Year	Per cent
1929	59.2	1952	30.1
1935-36	62.6	1953	29.0
1941	47.1	1954	30.2
1944	31.6	1955	27.3
——	——	1956	25.6
1946	32.3	1957	26.0
1947	34.9	1958	26.7
——	——	1959	25.9
——	——	1960	25.4
1950	34.5	1961	25.3
1951	31.4	1962	23.9

Source: *Survey of Current Business* (April 1964), p. 11.

affluence appears most conspicuous, we become increasingly concerned about poverty.

What is meant by poverty? The measure is a level of economic welfare inferior to a socially acceptable minimum standard.[4]
Such a definition of poverty is a relative, not an absolute, one. Let
us see why. Arbitrarily taking a figure of $3,000 income for con-
suming units as a line below which poverty exists, Table 23 shows
what percentage of consuming units have incomes of less than that
amount. Since these figures are given in dollars of constant value
(1954 dollars), they give a pretty clear notion of how the percentage of units below this level has really fallen. It stands at almost 60
per cent on 1929 and rises during the Depression as we would
expect; thereafter, it falls consistently at a rate of a little less than

[4] I have taken this definition and some of the subsequent analysis from
an unpublished paper by Harry Johnson titled "Unemployment and Poverty,"
presented at a conference on Poverty Amidst Affluence, at West Virginia,
May 5, 1965. I have also benefited from several unpublished papers on poverty
by Robert Lampman.

1 per cent per year. If it were to continue at this rate, then presumably in another twenty years no poverty at all would exist. But if we take our criterion back as far as 1900, we find that with the exception of a very small percentage, all Americans were poverty stricken. Moreover, an arbitrary level such as $3,000 would exceed average family income in almost every country in the world. While an absolute figure for the U.S. suggests the rapid elimination of poverty, a relative definition of poverty indicates that it is a much more stubborn problem. Since the share of income going to the lowest 20 per cent of consuming units has stayed relatively constant in the past 25 years, varying between 4 per cent and 5 per cent of national income, the problem is to increase the percentage of national income going to this group.

One major cause of their relative poverty is the size of their families, the number of individuals dependent on the income of the earning unit. This important factor invalidates any arbitrary measure such as a $3,000 maximum income. For young, individual earners, a couple just beginning their careers, or old couples, the $3,000 level may be very satisfactory, well above poverty; for a large family, even a higher income may leave them poverty stricken.

The other broad factor determining relative poverty has three major sources: (1) failure of the economy to provide enough jobs for everyone—that is, unemployment; (2) inability of people to contribute enough services to earn an income above the poverty line; people who lack skills, knowledge, or mental ability to earn adequately; and (3) restrictions on opportunity. The last difficulty is largely a case of discrimination, racial discrimination by far the most evident but certainly not the only source. Discrimination against the old and discrimination against women are important additional sources of poverty. Throughout our historical experience, all three of these sources have been important. Our eras of depression have been those in which unemployment has been particularly significant. Discrimination, and especially racial discrimination, has been an important source of poverty over a long period of time and still stubbornly resists change.[5] The widespread and

[5] Negroes have increased their incomes with the over-all growth but have not significantly closed the gap that separates them from whites of equal skills.

continuing development of the public education system in America has perhaps been the main line of attack against the second source of poverty and undoubtedly an important one.

The record of the past twenty years provides a basis for cautious optimism that we may possess the knowledge to prevent large-scale unemployment as a result of prolonged depressions. The systematic analysis of sources of poverty should enable us to separate well-meaning but misguided policies that are ineffective or that even exacerbate poverty—such as minimum wage laws—from policies that may provide a sound basis for its reduction—such as raising the productivity of labor by retraining and abolishing all forms of discrimination on the part of employers and trade unions.

The growth of the American economy is an unrivaled success story. We have attained an average level of economic well-being beyond the dreams and most optimistic forecasts of our early forebears. We shall never be without economic problems, but, the difference from the past lies in the resources now at our command and the knowledge with which we can attack them. The existence of poverty in this country of plenty is a good challenge.

SELECTIVE BIBLIOGRAPHY

This brief bibliography is confined to the major trends and issues dealt with in the individual chapters and is primarily a source for new research in United States economic history.

CHAPTER I

Fishlow, Albert, "Review of *Trends in the American Economy in the Nineteenth Century*" (ed. William N. Parker), *Journal of Economic History*, XXII, No. 2 (1962), 71-80.

Fogel, Robert W., *Railroads and American Economic Growth: Essays in Econometric History*. Baltimore: The Johns Hopkins Press, 1964, chaps. i and vi.

———, "The Reunification of Economic History with Economic Theory," *American Economic Review, Papers and Proceedings*, LV, No. 2 (1965), 92-97.

Hempel, Carl G., "The Function of General Laws in History," *Journal of Philosophy*, XXXIX, No. 2 (1942), 35-48; reprinted in Patrick Gardiner, *Theories of History; Readings From Classical and Contemporary Sources*. New York: The Free Press of Glencoe, Ill., 1959, pp. 344-56.

Meyer, John R. and Alfred H. Conrad, "Economic Theory, Statistical Inference and Economic History," *Journal of Economic History*, XVII, No. 4 (1957), 524-54.

North, Douglass C., "Quantitative Research in American Economic

History," *American Economic Review*, XLIII, No. 1, Part 1 (1963), 128-30.

————, "The State of Economic History, *American Economic Review, Papers and Proceedings*, LV, No. 2 (1965), 86-91.

CHAPTER 2

The main source of statistical information is U.S. Bureau of the Census, *Historical Statistics of the United States, Colonial Times to 1957.* Washington: Government Printing Office, 1960.

Goldsmith, Raymond, testimony before the United States Congress, Joint Economic Commitee, printed in "Employment, Growth, and The Price Level," 86th Cong. 1st Sess., Part II (1959). Washington: Government Printing Office, 1959.

Kuznets, Simon S., ed., *Population Redistribution and Economic Growth, United States, 1870-1950* (2 vols.). Philadelphia: The American Philosophical Society, 1957-1960.

Parker, William N., ed., *Trends in the American Economy in the Nineteenth Century.* NBER Studies in Income and Wealth, XXIV. Princeton, N.J.: Princeton University Press, 1960.

Perloff, Harvey S. et. al., *Regions, Resources, and Economic Growth.* Baltimore: published for Resources for the Future by the Johns Hopkins Press, 1960.

CHAPTER 3

The main statistics can be found in the Colonial section of *Historical Statistics of the United States, Colonial Times to 1957.* Washington: Government Printing Office, 1960.

Harper, Lawrence A., "The Effect of the Navigation Acts on the Thirteen Colonies," in R. B. Morris, ed., *The Era of the American Revolution.* New York: Columbia University Press, 1939, pp. 3-39.

Shepherd, James, "A Balance of Payments for the Thirteen Colonies, 1768-1772: A Summary," *Journal of Economic History*, XXV, No. 4 (1965).

————, "A Balance of Payments for the Thirteen Colonies, 1768-1772," Unpublished doctoral dissertation, University of Washington, 1965.

Thomas, Robert Paul, "A Quantitative Approach to the Study of the Effects of British Imperial Policy upon Colonial Welfare: Some Preliminary Findings," *Journal of Economic History*, XXV, No. 4 (1965).

CHAPTER 4

Bjork, Gordon C., "The Weaning of the American Economy: Independence, Market Changes, and Economic Development," *Journal of Economic History*, XXIV, No. 4 (1964), 541-60.

Fishlow, Albert, Discussion of foregoing article; *Journal of Economic History*, XXIV, No. 4 (1964), 561-66.

CHAPTER 5

Kuznets, Simon S., "National Income Estimates for the Period Prior to 1870," *Income and Wealth of the United States, Trends and Structures* (ed. Simon S. Kuznets). Cambridge, England: Bowes & Bowes, 1952.

North, Douglass C., "Early National Income Estimates of the United States," *Economic Development and Cultural Change*, IX, No. 3 (1961), 387-96.

————, *The Economic Growth of the United States, 1790-1860*. Englewood Cliffs, N.J.: Prentice-Hall, Inc., 1961. Part I, 1790-1814, pp. 1-58.

Parker, William N. and Franklee Whartenby, "The Growth of Output before 1840," *Trends in the American Economy in the Nineteenth Century* (ed. William N. Parker). NBER Studies in Income and Wealth, XXIV. Princeton, N.J.: Princeton University Press, 1960, pp. 191-212.

Taylor, George Rogers, "American Economic Growth Before 1840: An Exploratory Essay," *Journal of Economic History*, XXIV, No. 4 (1964), 427-44.

————, "The National Economy before and after the Civil War," *Economic Change in the Civil War Era* (ed. David T. Gilchrist and W. Davis Lewis). Greenville, Del.: Eleutherian Mills-Hagley Foundation, 1965, pp. 1-22.

CHAPTER 6

Gallman, Robert E., "Commodity Output, 1839-1899," in *Trends in the American Economy in the Nineteenth Century* (ed. William N. Parker). NBER Studies in Income and Wealth, XXIV. Princeton, N.J.: Princeton University Press, 1960.

North, Douglass C., "Capital Formation in the United States during the Early Period of Industrialization: A Re-examination of the Issues." 2nd International Conference of Economic History. Paris: Mouton and Co., 1965.

————, *The Economic Growth of the United States, 1790-1860*. Englewood Cliffs, N.J.: Prentice-Hall, Inc., 1961. Part II, 1815-1860, pp. 61-215.

Rostow, W. W., ed., *The Economics of Take-off into Sustained Growth*. Proceedings of a conference held by the International Economic Association. New York: St. Martin's Press, Inc., 1964.

————, *The Stages of Economic Growth: A Non-Communist Manifesto*. Cambridge, England: Cambridge University Press, 1960.

CHAPTER 7

Conrad, Alfred H. and John Meyer, "The Economics of Slavery in the Ante-Bellum South," *Journal of Political Economy*, LXVI, No. 2 (1958), 95-130.

Easterlin, Richard A., "Regional Income Trends, 1840-1950," *American Economic History* (ed. Seymour E. Harris). New York: McGraw-Hill Book Company, 1961, pp. 525-47.

Evans, Robert, Jr., "The Economics of American Negro Slavery," *Aspects of Labor Economics* (ed. H. Gregg Lewis). Conference of Universities-NBER. Princeton, N.J.: Princeton University Press, 1962, pp. 184-243.

Sutch, Richard, "The Profitability of Ante-Bellum Slavery—Revisited." *Southern Economic Journal*, XXXI, No. 4 (1965), 365-77.

Yasuba, Yasukichi, "The Profitability and Viability of Plantation Slavery in the United States," *Economics Studies Quarterly* (1961).

CHAPTER 8

Fogel, Robert W., *The Union Pacific Railroad: A Case in Premature Enterprise*. Baltimore: The Johns Hopkins Press, 1960.

Goodrich, Carter, and others, *Canals and American Economic Growth*. New York: Columbia University Press, 1960.

Griliches, Zvi, "Research Costs and Social Returns: Hybrid Corn and Related Innovations," *Journal of Political Economy*, LXVI, No. 5 (1958), 419-31.

Ransom, Roger L., "Canals and Development: A Discussion of the Issues," *American Economic Review, Papers and Proceedings*, LIV, No. 3 (1964), 365-76.

Schultz, Theodore W., *The Economic Organization of Agriculture*. New York: McGraw-Hill Book Company, 1953.

CHAPTER 9

Fishlow, Albert, *Railroads and the Transformation of the Ante-Bellum Economy*. Cambridge, Mass., Harvard University Press, 1965.

Fogel, Robert W., *Railroads and American Economic Growth: Essays in Econometric History*. Baltimore: The Johns Hopkins Press, 1964.

North, Douglass C., "Ocean Freight Rates and Economic Development, 1750-1913," *Journal of Economic History*, XVIII, No. 4 (1958), 537-55.

———, "The Role of Transportation in the Economic Development of North America." Paper presented to *The International Congress of the Historical Sciences*, Vienna, August 1965, and published in

Les grandes voies maritimes dans le monde, XVe-XIXe siècles. Paris: SEVPEN, 1965.

CHAPTER 10

The essential research has yet to be done. The best general source of the extensive literature by historians is Carstensen, Vernon, ed., *The Public Lands.* Madison: University of Wisconsin Press, 1963.

Bogue, Allan G. and Margaret B. Bogue, "Profits and the Frontier Land Speculator," *Journal of Economic History,* XVIII, No. 1 (1957), 1-24.

Fogel, Robert W., *The Union Pacific Railroad: A Case in Premature Enterprise.* Baltimore: The Johns Hopkins Press, 1960.

CHAPTER 11

Bogue, Allan G., *From Prairie to Cornbelt, Farming on the Illinois and Iowa Prairies in the Nineteenth Century.* Chicago: University of Chicago Press, 1963.

———, *Money at Interest: The Farm Mortgage on the Middle Border.* Ithaca: Cornell University Press, 1955.

Bowman, John D., *Trends in Midwestern Land Values, 1879-1914.* Unpublished doctoral dissertation, Yale University, 1964.

Rasmussen, Wayne D., "The Impact of Technological Change on American Agriculture, 1862-1962," *Journal of Economic History,* XXII, No. 4 (1962), 578-91.

Rothstein, Morton, "America in the International Rivalry for the British Wheat Market," *Mississippi Valley Historical Review,* XLVII, No. 3 (1960), 401-18.

CHAPTER 12

The most important general sources for this period are the National Bureau of Economic Research Studies. Also Peter Temin's work is a pioneering case of analytical economic history of an important industry.

Davis, Lance, "The Investment Market, 1870-1914: The Evolution of a National Market," *Journal of Economic History,* XXV, No. 3 (1965).

Rees, Albert, *Real Wages in Manufacturing, 1890-1914.* Princeton, N.J.: Princeton University Press, 1961.

Temin, Peter, *Iron and Steel in Nineteenth-Century America: An Economic Inquiry.* Cambridge, Mass.: M.I.T. Press, 1964.

CHAPTER 13

Brown, E. Cary, "Fiscal Policy in the 'Thirties: A Reappraisal," *American Economic Review,* XLVI, No. 5 (1956), 857-79.

Friedman, Milton, and Anna Schwartz, *A Monetary History of the United States, 1867-1960*. Princeton, N.J.: Princeton University Press, 1963.

Kravis, Irving B., "Relative Income Shares in Fact and Theory," *American Economic Review*, XLIX, No. 5 (1959), 917-49.

Kuznets, Simon S. assisted by Elizabeth Jenks, *Shares of Upper Income Groups in Income and Saving*. New York: NBER, 1953.

Lampman, Robert J., *The Share of Top Wealth-Holders in National Wealth, 1922-1956*. A study by the NBER. Princeton, N.J.: Princeton University Press, 1962.

Moore, Geoffrey H., "Secular Changes in the Distribution of Income," *American Economic Review, Papers and Proceedings*, XLII, No. 2 (1952), 527-44.

CHAPTER 14

Becker, Gary S., *The Economics of Discrimination*. Chicago: University of Chicago Press, 1957.

Denison, Edward F., *The Sources of Economic Growth in the United States and the Alternatives Before Us*, Supplementary Paper No. 13. New York: Committee for Economic Development, 1962.

Stigler, George J., "The Economist and the State," *American Economic Review*, LV, No. 1 (1965), 1-18.

INDEX